DISCARDED:
OUTDATED, REDUNDANT
MATERIAL

W9-DDA-574

305.40942 SWI
Swisher, Clarice,
Women of Victorian
 England /

PALM BEACH COUNTY
LIBRARY SYSTEM
3650 SUMMIT BLVD
WEST PALM BEACH, FLORIDA 33406

DISCARDED:
OUTDATED, REDUNDANT
MATERIAL

Women in History

Women of Victorian England

Clarice Swisher

LUCENT BOOKS

An imprint of Thomson Gale, a part of The Thomson Corporation

THOMSON

GALE

Detroit • New York • San Francisco • San Diego • New Haven, Conn. • Waterville, Maine • London • Munich

For Marion

© 2005 Thomson Gale, a part of The Thomson Corporation.

Thomson and Star Logo are trademarks and Gale and Lucent Books are registered trademarks used herein under license.

For more information, contact
Lucent Books
27500 Drake Rd.
Farmington Hills, MI 48331-3535
Or you can visit our Internet site at http://www.gale.com

ALL RIGHTS RESERVED.
No part of this work covered by the copyright hereon may be reproduced or used in any form or by any means—graphic, electronic, or mechanical, including photocopying, recording, taping, Web distribution, or information storage retrieval systems—without the written permission of the publisher.

Every effort has been made to trace the owners of copyrighted material.

LIBRARY OF CONGRESS CATALOGING-IN-PUBLICATION DATA

Swisher, Clarice, 1933–
  Women of Victorian England / by Clarice Swisher.
    p. cm. — (Women in history)
  Includes bibliographical references and index.
  ISBN 1-59018-571-4 (lib. : alk. paper)
    1. Women—England—History—19th century—Juvenile literature. 2. Women—England—Social conditions—19th century—Juvenile literature. 3. Sex role—England—History—19th century—Juvenile literature. I. Title. II. Series: Women in history (San Diego, Calif.)
    HQ1599.E5S95 2004
    305.4'0942'09034--dc22

                        2004010848

Printed in the United States of America

Contents

Foreword   4

Introduction: The Strength and Grit of Victorian Women   6

Chapter 1:
The Middle Class Determines Ideal Roles for Women   10

Chapter 2:
Women as Pieceworkers and Shopkeepers   23

Chapter 3:
Women in a Life of Service   34

Chapter 4:
Women Employed in Industry   47

Chapter 5:
Women Philanthropists and Reformers   60

Chapter 6:
Women Entertainers   73

Chapter 7:
Women Writers   84

Notes   97

For Further Reading   101

Works Consulted   103

Index   106

Picture Credits   111

About the Author   112

Foreword

The story of the past as told in traditional historical writings all too often leaves the impression that if men are not the only actors in the narrative, they are assuredly the main characters. With a few notable exceptions, males were the political, military, and economic leaders in virtually every culture throughout recorded time. Since traditional historical scholarship focuses on the public arenas of government, foreign relations, and commerce, the actions and ideas of men—or at least of powerful men—are naturally at the center of conventional accounts of the past.

In the last several decades, however, many historians have abandoned their predecessors' emphasis on "great men" to explore the past "from the bottom up," a phenomenon that has had important consequences for the study of women's history. These social historians, as they are known, focus on the day-to-day experiences of the "silent majority"—those people typically omitted from conventional scholarship because they held relatively little political or economic sway within their societies. In the new social history, members of ethnic and racial minorities, factory workers, peasants, slaves, children, and women are no longer relegated to the background but are placed at the very heart of the narrative.

Around the same time social historians began broadening their research to include women and other previously neglected elements of society, the feminist movement of the late 1960s and 1970s was also bringing unprecedented attention to the female heritage. Feminists hoped that by examining women's past experiences, contemporary women could better understand why and how gender-based expectations had developed in their societies, as well as how they might reshape inherited—and typically restrictive—economic, social, and political roles in the future.

Today, some four decades after the feminist and social history movements gave new impetus to the study of women's history, there is a rich and continually growing body of work on all aspects of women's lives in the past. The Lucent Books Women in History series draws upon this abundant and diverse literature to introduce students to women's experiences within a variety of past cultures and time periods in terms of the distinct roles they filled. In their capacities as workers, activists, and artists, women exerted significant influence on important events whether they conformed to or broke from traditional roles. The Women in History titles depict extraordinary women who managed to attain positions of influence in their male-dominated societies, including such celebrated heroines as the feisty medieval queen Eleanor of Aquitaine, the brilliant propagandist of the American Revolution Mercy Otis Warren, and the courageous African American activist of the Civil War era Harriet Tubman. Included as well are the stories of the ordinary—and often overlooked—women of the past who also helped shape their societies myriad ways—moral, intellectual, and economic—without straying far from customary gender roles: the housewives and mothers, schoolteachers and church volunteers, midwives and nurses and wartime camp followers.

In this series, readers will discover that many of these unsung women took more significant parts in the great political and social upheavals of their day than has often been recognized. In *Women of the American Revolution,* for example, students will learn how American housewives assumed a crucial role in helping the Patriots win the war against Britain. They accomplished this by planting and harvesting fields, producing and trading goods, and doing whatever else was necessary to maintain the family farm

or business in the absence of their soldier husbands despite the heavy burden of housekeeping and child-care duties they already bore. By their self-sacrificing actions, competence, and ingenuity, these anonymous heroines not only kept their families alive, but kept the economy of their struggling young nation going as well during eight long years of war.

Each volume in this series contains generous commentary from the works of respected contemporary scholars, but the Women in History series particularly emphasizes quotations from primary sources such as diaries, letters, and journals whenever possible to allow the women of the past to speak for themselves. These firsthand accounts not only help students to better understand the dimensions of women's daily spheres—the work they did, the organizations they belonged to, the physical hardships they faced—but also how they viewed themselves and their actions in the light of their society's expectations for their sex.

The distinguished American historian Mary Beard once wrote that women have always been a "force in history." It is hoped that the books in this series will help students to better appreciate the vital yet often little-known ways in which women of the past have shaped their societies and cultures.

Introduction:
The Strength and Grit of Victorian Women

The Victorian era in England did not begin with the coronation of Queen Victoria in 1837 nor did it end suddenly upon her death in 1901. The attitudes and practices that characterize Victorian England began to develop with the advent of the Industrial Revolution near the end of the 1700s and remained largely in place until the outbreak of World War I in 1914. During this span of more than a century, England changed from an agricultural to an industrial economy, from a rural to an urban society, and from a nation dominated by the aristocracy to one dominated by the middle class. All of these changes affected women and caused hardships for them, but they responded with strength and grit. In a society still dominated by men, they applied intelligence and creativity to solve problems, and they fought to protect their own well-being in ways women had never done before.

Hardship and Domination

The changes England saw during the Victorian era imposed psychological, economic, and physical hardships on everyone, but particularly on women. For example, radical changes in patterns of landownership caused upheavals in agricultural life in England. Vast tracts of public land were sold to wealthy individuals. Now unable to rent land for low costs, previously independent farmers were forced to take jobs as hourly agricultural workers or move to town and work in factories. Both options caused uncertainty and psychological distress. Whatever choice working-class people made, they had difficulty supporting themselves and their families on what they were paid since this was a time when employers felt free to exploit workers in pursuit of wealth. This attitude particularly impacted women in agriculture, mining, manufacturing, and domestic service. These individuals, if they were single, earned barely enough to survive. Married women, meanwhile, worked to supplement their husbands' low wages. No matter what the job, women endured hard physical work. On farms, many swung a sickle, harvesting grain from dawn to dusk. In mines, they crawled on hands and knee, pulling carts of coal through the mine tunnels. In factories, they stood for hours at machines, producing the same item again and again. In homes, they carried their employers' water and wrung heavy wet laundry by hand.

In addition, through most of the early Victorian period women had little or no control over their fate. Men dominated women at home, and male work masters

The Victorian era in England is named after Queen Victoria, who ruled from 1837 to 1901.

dominated female employees on farms and in mines and factories. Men also supervised female servants in households. Until Britain's Parliament passed laws protecting women from the worst abuses, they endured poverty and hardship that people in times since find almost incomprehensible. Moreover, women had no legal rights. Treated as property themselves, women had no rights to own anything, no rights to divorce abusive husbands, and no rights to custody of their children in separations. They had no means of preventing exploitation by greedy employers. Factory owners said openly that women could be paid less than men and could be forced to work longer hours. Victorian women did not simply endure such treatment, however. They used their intelligence and creativity to circumvent obstacles and overcome hardships.

Managing the System

Since women lived under a political and social system that controlled them, it is antonishing that they were able to overcome their difficulties. Victorian women cleverly found ways to fulfill their own real needs and, at the same time, appear to conform to the system. For example, one woman, whose husband insisted on reading all of her letters before she mailed them, would wait until he left on business and then write and mail her letters before he came home.

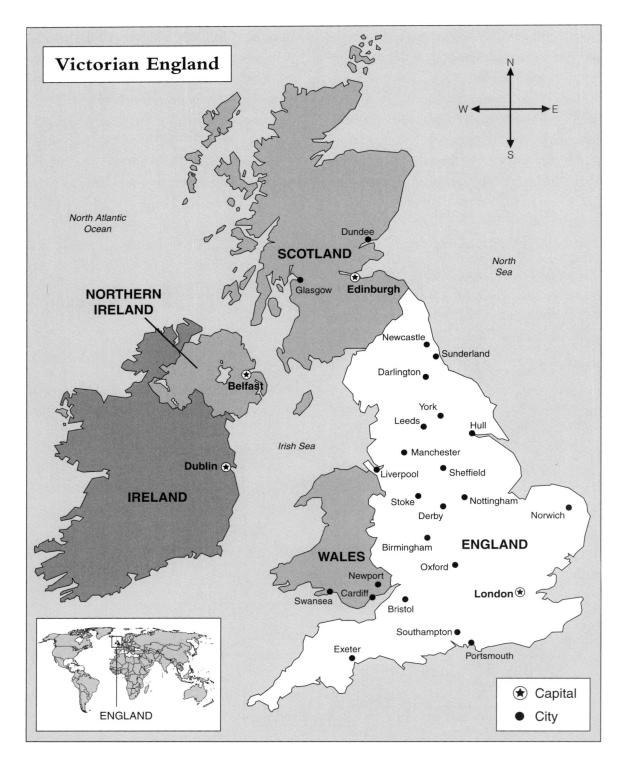

Victorian England

North Atlantic
Ocean

SCOTLAND

Dundee

**NORTHERN
IRELAND**

North
Sea

Glasgow
Edinburgh

Belfast

Newcastle
Sunderland

Darlington

York
Leeds
Hull

Irish Sea

Manchester

Dublin

Liverpool
Sheffield

IRELAND

Stoke
Nottingham
Norwich

Derby

WALES

Birmingham
ENGLAND

Oxford

Newport
London

Cardiff
Swansea
Bristol

Exeter
Southampton
Portsmouth

ENGLAND

⊛ Capital
● City

Since the social system disapproved of women working for pay, those who needed to supplement the family income worked privately at needlework in their homes and sold their work secretly. Because women were denied education and were discouraged from thinking for themselves, Victorian women found creative ways to use their intelligence and talents in the few ways society would permit. They organized projects for helping the poor. They used their talents in musical and theatrical entertainment, and they wrote poetry, novels, and articles for magazines and newspapers.

Fighting Back

Finally, women fought back against the system that oppressed them. They fought for their legal rights. Organizers of these campaigns were either single women or they were married ones with progessive-minded husbands who supported them. In addition to organizing protests, these leaders gave public speeches. They wrote articles in periodicals and designed and passed out pamphlets promoting their cause. Wealthy women gave money to support the campaigns. Women with political connections lobbied for Parliament to pass bills to protect women. They wrote letters to members of Parliament, sometimes signing with men's names to increase the chances that they would be read. These activists helped working women form unions and in one case help organize a strike.

There were those, however, who disagreed with the reformers and subscribed to the submissive-woman idea. Foremost among them was Queen Victoria. Historian Richard D. Altick quotes the queen's response to the feminists:

> "The Queen," wrote Victoria in her regal third-person style, "is most anxious to enlist everyone who can speak or write to join in checking this mad wicked folly of Women's Rights, with all its attendant horrors, on which her poor, feeble sex is bent, forgetting every sense of womanly feeling and propriety." [1]

With so formidable an opponent to the granting of equal rights, women across the social spectrum would have to rely not just on the goodwill of Britain's leaders but also on their own strength and grit to survive.

Chapter 1:
The Middle Class Determines Ideal Roles for Women

❦

In Victorian England, the Industrial Revolution brought profound economic and social changes. The British economy had expanded enormously, giving rise to a large and powerful middle class, dominated by men. As members of the middle class earned more, they emulated the upper class in matters of style. But the middle class differed from the upper class by placing stricter emphasis on morality, religion, and the role of women. Thanks to its size, the middle class and its values came to be seen as the ideal for the family in general and for women in particular. In *Victorian Women,* Joan Perkin explains:

> This patriarchal family was regarded by many people as the essential building block of a civilized society. The Victorian family—by which was meant the affluent middle-class family, of course—won for itself a reputation as a noble institution upon whose continuance depended all that was fine and stable in Britain. [2]

Because women were expected to be partners (albeit unequal ones) in such families, marriage was the goal of nearly all Victorian women. Most had no other way to attain economic security, and being unmarried became a stigma to be avoided. Girls were expected to focus their attention in their late teens on getting a husband. In 1844 writer Ann Richelieu observed that if a man gave even slight attention to a young girl, it aroused hopes for serious attention and started gossip about a love affair. Most Victorian women complied with this convention and became wives.

The Ideal Submissive Wife

Foremost among middle-class ideals was the notion that a wife was to be subservient to her husband. The ideal middle-class wife was expected to adopt her husband's values since he was the family patriarch. Such an ideal placed little or no value on individuality. Perkin explains Victorian men's idea of the perfect wife:

Men's idea was of a decoratively idle, sexually passive woman, pure of heart, religious and self-sacrificing. The most popular image was of an "angel in the house," an ivy-like wife who was also a doting and self-abnegating mother, clinging to her husband on whom she was totally dependent. [3]

As a dependent, subservient wife, she was expected to display little knowledge of the affairs of the day or to hold ideas other than her husband's. In public, she remained silent on serious subjects and smiled agreeably when her husband spoke. Popular writer Sarah Stickney Ellis, who was also a clergyman's wife, said in 1830, "The first thing of importance is to be content to be inferior to men, inferior in mental power in the same proportion that you are inferior in bodily strength." [4]

Many men, in fact, believed that women were mentally very different from themselves. Physiologist Alexander Walker explained the supposed differences in 1840 in his book *Women Physiologically Considered*:

It is evident that the man, possessing reasoning faculties, muscular power, and courage to employ it, is qualified for being a protector: the woman, being little capable of reasoning, feeble, and timid, requires protection. Under the circumstances, the man naturally governs; the woman as naturally obeys. [5]

Being uninformed extended to the functioning of their own bodies. In particular, women were expected to be ignorant about sexual matters and reproduction. Many women could fulfill this expectation because they had little opportunity to learn about sex. Middle-class adults encouraged ignorance about sex, assuming that this kept their daughters pure. At the same time, women were expected to be compliant but indifferent about sexual relations with their husbands. Some easily adopted such indifference. One woman admitted that she was happy when, as time went on, her husband came to her bedroom less often. When she did hear him coming to her door, she said she closed her eyes and thought about England.

Symbolizing Wealth

Whatever else her husband might demand, an ideal middle-class wife was expected to enhance the social status of the family, an expectation she fulfilled through her activities and her dress. The goal was for her to appear idle, that it was unnecessary for her to do housework because her husband could afford to hire servants to do it. In lieu of doing household chores, she was supposed to call on friends and relatives, shop, or gather female friends in her parlor to do fancy needlework.

On all social occasions, whether with women friends during the day or social events in the evening with her husband,

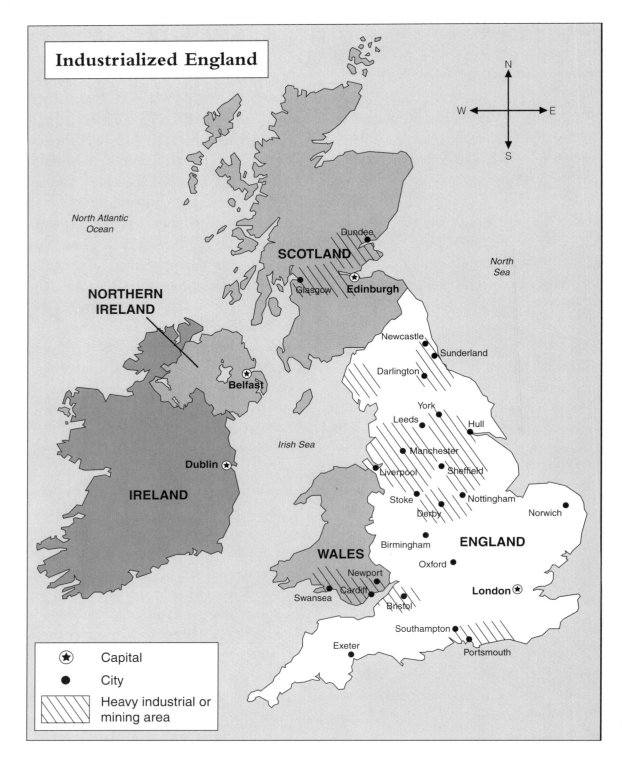

Industrialized England

North Atlantic Ocean

SCOTLAND

Dundee

Glasgow • **Edinburgh** ⍟

NORTHERN IRELAND

North Sea

Belfast ⍟

Newcastle •
• Sunderland

Darlington •

York •

Leeds •
• Hull

Irish Sea

Manchester •

Liverpool •
• Sheffield

Dublin ⍟

Stoke •
• Nottingham

Derby •
• Norwich

IRELAND

Birmingham •

WALES

Oxford •

ENGLAND

Newport •
Swansea • Cardiff •

London ⍟

Bristol •

Southampton •

Exeter •
• Portsmouth

Legend:
- ⍟ Capital
- • City
- ▨ Heavy industrial or mining area

N / W — E / S (compass)

the ideal wife dressed in a fashion that conveyed an aura of wealth and status. Ideally, the message was that the family had unlimited money to spend on new fashions and a variety of styles. In an essay, modern social historian Helene Roberts captures the goal of dress:

To fulfill the needs of conspicuous consumption, dress must look very costly, be made from rich fabrics, and have expensive decorations. A rapidly changing fashion fulfills the dictates of conspicuous waste, for garments must be discarded as out of fashion long before they are worn out. Conspicuous leisure may be demonstrated by wearing garments that preclude physical labor and necessitate the help of servants in dressing and maintaining a wardrobe. [6]

In this early-twentieth-century portrait, an elegantly dressed Victorian woman relaxes in an oversized chair.

Most dress styles, even though they varied, were decorated with finely crafted ruffles, bows, embroidery, or artificial flowers. Beautiful fabrics and quality decorations of this sort were expensive and, therefore, indicated the wealth of the family.

Women were expected to uphold this ideal despite their actual circumstances. Not surprisingly, the more money her husband earned, the more easily a Victorian wife could fulfill the role of ideal wife. The upper economic bracket of the middle class, consisting of businessmen and lawyers who had incomes of one thousand pounds or more per year was the exception, although at just over 40 percent, theirs was a substantial segment. In the middle of the middle class were the owners of small businesses, about 10 percent, who earned one hundred to three hundred pounds per year. The lower middle class, mostly shopkeepers and clerks, earned less than one hundred pounds per year. This segment composed some 49 percent of the middle class.

An Argument for Women's Education

In a paper read before the Social Science Association in October 1871, Mrs. William Grey advocates education and work for girls and women. In this excerpt, she urges parents to educate girls and instill in them a desire to do paid or volunteer work. This excerpt is reprinted in *Free and Ennobled,* edited by Carol Bauer and Lawrence Ritt.

So long as marriage is . . . the only aim of a girl's life, and her education regulated with the sole view of making her pleasing to marrying men, so long will all attempts at improvement fail, except with the few [girls] capable of rising above the average tone of thought and feeling. . . . All who hold the higher and truer view [must] urge upon parents, and upon society, that marriage should not be the first object of a woman's life, any more than of a man's: that girls should be trained from childhood, to the idea that they, like their brothers, must take their share of the work of life; that their education should prepare them by good intellectual and moral habits, to perform it well;—that they should be not only allowed, but induced to work for their own maintenance, where the circumstances of their parents made an independent provision for them impossible, and that when those circumstances place them above the necessity of working for a provision, they should hold themselves bound to help, and train themselves to help efficiently in doing the unpaid work of the world, where the harvest is plentiful and the labourers so few.

In practical terms, about 59 percent of the middle class had insufficient resources to conform to middle-class standards. For the women, this circumstance required considerable talent for improvisation.

A Learned Role

Just as the upper-income women set the standard for dress among all middle-class women, so too did they provide the model of the ideal mother. Women were not, however, expected to possess an instinct for this role. To discover the best way to raise children, middle-class Victorian women turned to guidebooks. Historian Deborah Gorham explains:

> In order to be considered a good mother, a woman would not only be expected to devote time and effort to her role, she was expected to approach that role in a new way. Motherhood came to be defined as a skill that had to be learned, rather than as behaviour that could be acquired simply by contact with other women who had been mothers. As one historian has put it, motherhood was undergoing "modernisation" in the nineteenth century, and the modernisation of motherhood implied a willingness to seek advice and information from those who were considered to have an expertise based on systematic knowledge.[7]

From the 1840s on, advice was readily available in handbooks and journals, and the market for such literature increased in the following decades.

A Concern for Health

There was plenty of opportunity to put such advice to the test. The ideal Victorian wife was expected to have babies, six or seven if she lived during the early part of the nineteenth century; women living during the later part of the century still were expected to have four or five. Simply bearing so many children was an enormous burden. Giving birth was painful, and there was little that doctors could—or would—do to alleviate pain. Eventually, chloroform, a crude but effective anesthetic, came to be used. Not until after 1853, however, when Queen Victoria allowed her doctor to administer chloroform during the birth of her eighth child, did this type of relief from the pain of childbirth become routinely used.

A Victorian mother had to be particularly concerned about her children's health. Doctors at the time had few ways to treat disease, so even a cold, if it developed into pneumonia, could be deadly. In 1866, *Ward and Lock's Home Book* had this advice for dressing daughters in winter to prevent colds:

> The following dress for a little girl in winter is *not a catch a cold* one, and is

sensibly considered—warm woollen stockings, hand-knitted in fine, soft, pretty wool . . . thick double-soled boots, high up the leg . . . a chemise of good, but somewhat stout long-cloth, drawers . . . in the form of knickerbockers . . . a scarlet flannel petticoat. [8]

When a child fell ill, it was the mother's job to do the nursing, so advice manuals also made suggestions for ways to look after a sick youngster. In 1861 writer Isabella Beeton recommended that mothers learn from observation and reading. She said that the main requirements are "good temper, compassion for suffering, sympathy with sufferers, which most women worthy of the name possess, neat-handedness, quiet manners, love of order, and cleanliness." [9]

Such advice belies how trying it could be for a mother nursing a seriously ill child. For example, Annie Wood Besant writes in her autobiography how her baby daughter Mabel was near death for weeks with whooping cough. Besant held the baby on her lap day and night. Eventually the baby recovered, but the experience had a profound effect on the mother. She writes:

Not unnaturally, when the child was out of danger, I collapsed from sheer exhaustion, and I lay in bed for a week. But an important change of mind dated from those silent weeks with a dying child on my knees. There had grown in my mind a feeling of angry resentment against the God who had been for weeks, as I thought, torturing my helpless baby. . . . To me he [God] was not an abstract idea, but a living reality, and all my mother-heart rose up in rebellion against this person in whom I believed, and whose individual finger I saw in my baby's agony. [10]

Mothers as Teachers

Annie Besant's loss of faith must have been difficult for her since ideally religious faith in general and Christian belief specifically lay at the heart of middle-class family life. A mother had the job of instilling religion and morality into her children's lives. In *Woman's Mission,* published in 1839, Sarah Lewis suggested that religious faith came naturally to women:

They are naturally disposed to reverence, to worship, to self-sacrifice, for the sake of a beloved object. These peculiar qualities, accompanied by unenlightened intellect and narrow views, lead them to minute devotional practices, to the unlimited indulgence of religious sensibility, and partial unintelligent obedience. Grafted

A Victorian mother shows her daughter how to brush her hair properly in this late-nineteenth-century painting.

her children Bible stories, took them to church on Sunday, and encouraged their participation in family prayers and Bible readings. Moreover, she reinforced behaviors consistent with their religious instruction. These included obeying those in authority, working hard, acting unselfishly, and using proper and respectable language.

Closely associated with these behaviors was valuing orderliness and attention to detail, both qualities thought to be necessary for success in middle-class endeavors. Instilling orderliness fell to the mother from the time her children were very young. She taught these qualities by establishing routines, such as regular times for meals, dressing, and play. The dinner table served as a time for children to learn appropriate mealtime conversation and proper manners. Writer Geoffrey Eley quotes a guidebook explaining proper table manners that mothers were expected to teach:

on enlightened Christianity, they may accomplish—what may they *not* accomplish? . . . Let them deeply engrave these principles on the hearts of their children.[11]

To carry out her role as keeper of Christian values, the Victorian mother taught

Holding knife, spoon, and fork correctly will come to a child naturally, and it should not be forgotten that if the pudding-spoon and fork are grasped from beneath instead of from above, the awkward uplifting of the elbow will be avoided. When children have become too old to wear bibs, so important for the use of small boys and girls, they ought to be provided with table napkins, and shown when to use them—after taking soup, &c.: but they must not be allowed to rub their mouths continually, as some people are in the habit of doing. . . .

Children must not fidget at the table. They should sit upright, possibly resting the back on the bars of the chair behind them, but on no account lolling carelessly or leaning on the table. [12]

Thus, the mother who dressed her children properly, instilled moral values, and trained them to have polished manners fulfilled her duty and made her husband proud.

Teaching Gender and Class Distinctions

Finally, it was up to the middle-class mother to teach her sons to fulfill their roles as males and her daughters to be properly feminine. Mothers firmly directed the children's activities and insisted that girls learn household tasks while boys participate in rough activities. Girls played reserved games in the garden while boys

Victorian girls sing to the accompaniment of a piano in this English painting.

Women of Victorian England

competed on the athletic field. Gorham explains the reasons for the differences: "Boys had to be prepared to compete in the public sphere; girls had to be prepared, both as future mothers, and as representatives of their class."[13] Most girls saw the unfairness of the double standard for girls and boys. In *Wives of England,* published in 1843, Sarah Stickney Ellis said, "I never could imagine why little girls were to fetch and carry . . . while boys sat still and fancied themselves into lords of creation."[14] The girls were not, however, allowed to complain openly.

Middle-class mothers also instilled in their children awareness of class distinctions. It was acceptable to socialize with children of classes above them, even though upper-class children were rarely allowed to associate with them. Above all, middle-class children were to be kept apart from the working-class children, from whom, mothers thought, their children might learn bad morals. Perkin tells the story of Stella Davies, the daughter of a successful salesman, to illustrate how firmly mothers enforced class lines even late in the Victorian era. Davies

recalled living in Edwardian Manchester in a large house, with a maid of all work, "Fat Ellen." A street of working-class houses with lots of children ran the length of their garden but, she said, "We were not allowed to speak to them." Next door lived a wealthy Manchester merchant who employed servants and a nursemaid to look after his children, but they too "were not allowed to play with us."[15]

Keeping her children happy and training them properly for their future middle-class roles was a large undertaking for the ideal mother, who had her own role to play as wife.

The Ideal Homemaker

Victorian women found the greatest conflict between ideal and real life in their role as homemakers. It was simply a contradiction in terms to be idle and keep the ideal home, even when circumstances allowed a woman to be aided by a fleet of servants. In wealthy upper-middle-class homes with an array of servants, the homemaker met daily with the servants to clarify the tasks for the day. Among the servants were a housekeeper, cook, kitchen maid, butler, footman, valet, upper and under housemaids, lady's maid, maid of all work, laundry maid, nurse, and nursemaid. In 1861 advice columnist Isabella Beeton said that the mistress of the house resembled the commander of an army or the leader of a business. As manager, the homemaker hired and trained servants, arranged for their living quarters, organized household tasks, and oversaw the servants assigned to daily tasks.

A Working-Class Woman's Power

In the ideal Victorian family, the father held the position of authority, but, in reality, many women made the decisions. This excerpt from Elizabeth Roberts's book *A Woman's Place: An Oral History of Working-Class Women, 1890–1940* tells a story that illustrates a mother's power.

Did your father ever play sports when he was young?

He used to play when they were first married. . . . All the local lads used to play football on there and my dad was one of them. He would always play on a Saturday afternoon. My mother got fed up with this here as he was always going playing football. He would wear a pair of shorts. One weekend he said to my mother, "Where's my shorts? I can't find them and I'm going to play football." She said, "You're not playing football no more." She put them [the shorts] on the fire. He never played football any more.

Besides managing servants, the homemaker was responsible for the house and everything that took place within it. She purchased food and selected menus for the family dining. She planned the decor and purchased the furnishings, and she would redecorate when necessary in order to keep up with changing fashion. When the roof leaked or a window was broken, she saw that repairs were made. Considering all that was expected of a Victorian homemaker, she had little time to be idle.

In addition to managing the servants and the house, the ideal homemaker was expected to fulfill the family's social obligations. A woman would call on friends and neighbors who had births, marriages, or deaths in the family or who had given a party or picnic. She would take her calling card (a printed card with her name) to the home of the woman she was calling on, give the card to the servant who answered the door, and then wait to be admitted for a short visit if the woman was at home. Conversely, a woman at home was expected to receive either morning or afternoon callers.

Fulfilling the roles of ideal homemaker was hard enough for those who had money, but it was much harder for the majority, whose finances were inadequate for the middle-class lifestyle. To help them cope, most middle-class women had two or three servants, although some had only one. Paying for this help was often a challenge. Historian Jane Lewis notes:

The image of the perfect Victorian lady, to all intents and purposes decorative and idle, has been fractured by [writer Patricia] Branca's consideration of the attention to household budgeting and routine demanded of the large number of middle class wives responsible for making ends meet on between 100 [pounds] and 300 [pounds] a year.[16]

Though these lower-middle-class homemakers likely had smaller houses than the wealthier homemakers, they were still responsible for running the home. They solved the problem by doing much of the washing, cleaning, and cooking themselves with the help of their daughters and perhaps one servant.

Finally, the ideal homemaker was expected to create a place of domestic

In this mid-nineteenth-century painting, a Victorian woman plays the piano while her companion rests from playing the guitar.

bliss while walking a tightrope of contradictions. She was expected to serve others but never to show agitation or irritation or to expect appreciation. In her essay titled "Characteristics of Husbands," Sarah Stickney Ellis says, "As it is the natural characteristic of woman's love in its most refined, as well as its most practical development, to be perpetually doing something for the good or the happiness of the object of her affection, it is but reasonable that man's personal comfort should be studiously attended to."[17] Such advice did not mask the fact that some Victorian women recognized that they were being exploited. Perhaps Florence Nightingale expressed the role of the ideal middle-class Victorian woman most realistically in "The Household Prisoner" when she said:

> Women never have an half-hour in all their lives (excepting before and after anybody is up in the house) that they can call their own, without fear of offending or of hurting someone. Why do people sit up so late, or, more rarely, get up so early? Not because the day is not long enough, but because they have "no time in the day to themselves."[18]

Not All Conformed

In reality, not all middle-class families were patriarchal. There were husbands who wanted educated wives as their companions. Others encouraged their wives in their work, and some worked with their wives. For example, Anna Brownell Murphy Jameson was married to the lawyer Robert Jameson, who encouraged Anna to publish her first work, *The Diary of an Ennuyee.* She then traveled with her husband to Canada and described their journey in a memoir titled *Winter Studies and Summer Rambles in Canada.*

While many Victorian women strove to conform to the ideal, circumstances forced some to circumvent expectations or compromise them. Many upper-class women ignored the ideal role of wife, mother, and homemaker and lived as they had lived before the rise of the middle class. Other women were aware of the ideal role and wanted to be respectable, but for them the middle-class lifestyle remained an unattainable ideal.

Chapter 2:
Women as Pieceworkers and Shopkeepers

Victorian women knew about the middle-class ideal, according to which the wife supervised a fleet of servants, but only a minority of women actually lived according to this ideal. The majority of Victorian women had no choice but to take jobs in order to supplement the family income. Some worked in shops as clerks. Others worked as street vendors. Most, however, worked at home, producing small items for sale. Regardless of where a woman worked or what kind of work she did, all women received low pay.

Even for women whose husbands earned from one hundred to three hundred pounds per year—making them technically part of the middle class—some labor for pay was necessary in order for them to maintain the appearance of respectability. Indeed, this instinct for respectability in part determined where they worked. Work done at home was considered respectable, but going out to work in a factory was not. Social historian Jane Lewis says, "The influence of the domestic idyll of the wife staying at home managing the home and family and the husband going out to work to earn the family living was very strong. So too was the idea that a woman staying at home was respected more than one going out to work." [19] At home, women earned money doing piecework, which involved making various handmade items for which a woman was paid by the piece.

Needlework

The most popular form of piecework was needlework since women could combine this activity with fulfilling their duties as wife and mother. Needlework included lace making, glove stitching, knitting, straw plaiting (braiding straw for milliners), millinery (hat making), and sewing. Girls who expected to have to work someday learned these skills early, when they were in their teens. Some learned from their mothers at home. Eva Paine, who was learning lace making from her mother, said that the work was hard and caused

This painting shows a lace maker at work. Lace making and other needlework were popular forms of piecework during the Victorian era.

known as penny capitalists. They did the sewing for people who brought directions and fabric for any item they wanted made. Sometimes the orders came from government agencies. For example, one woman made suits for convicts. It took her a day and a half, working from nine in the morning until eleven at night, to complete one suit; for each suit she was paid the modern equivalent of about $1.25. Out of that she had to provide the thread and pay for a candle to provide light for her evening work. Another penny capitalist made nightcaps, children's chemises (loose-fitting undergarments), and cravats (bands of fabric worn around the neck as ties). She noted how the work was hard and the pay low:

I did seven chemises in a fortnight, and got 7s [about $15.00] for them. I have also made within this time one dozen white cravats for a shop; they are white corded-muslin cut across, and the very largest. I have 6d [about $1.10] a dozen for hemming them; I thought they would never have been done, there was so much work in them. Myself and daughter hemmed the dozen in a day. It was a day's very hard work. It was really such hard work that I cried over it. I was so ill, and we were wanting food so badly. [21]

pain in her hands and arms. Others attended what were known as cottage schools. In such schools students learned how arduous their work could be. Betty Yewsdale said of her Yorkshire knitting school, "We knit as hard as we can [because] the one who knits the slowest gets well thumped." [20] When these girls married, they had a skill they could use to supplement the family income should that be necessary.

Women who did needlework at home had their own small businesses and were

Not only was the work difficult, but doing it at home made it all the more difficult to complete the other domestic chores expected of Victorian women. Frances Place, a working-class woman, did her tailoring work in a small house. She said, "Nothing conduces so much to the degradation of . . . the woman, than her having to eat and drink and cook and wash and iron and transact all her domestic concerns in the room in which [the family] work."[22]

Some penny capitalists had better experiences in their work than others. In *Rural Rides,* writer and politician William Cobbett tells about a glove maker in rural England. She and her daughters made gloves while the men in the family worked in the fields. Cobbett says, "This is a great thing for the land where manufacturing

Hard Labor for Young Girls

Young girls worked long hours in dressmaking shops, especially when large numbers of dresses had been ordered for an upcoming ball. In this excerpt, Mrs. Gaskill describes the tired girls in a typical shop and the shop owner's gimmick to urge the girls to finish the dresses. The excerpt comes from the novel *Ruth* and is reprinted in *English Women in Life & Letters* by M. Phillips and W.S. Tomkinson.

Mrs. Mason was particularly desirous that here workwomen should exert themselves to-night, for on the next, the annual hunt-ball was to take place. It was the one gaiety of the town since the assize-balls had been discontinued. Many were the dresses she had promised should be sent home "without fail" the next morning; she had not let one slip through her fingers, for fear, if it did, it might fall into the hands of the rival dressmaker who had just established herself in the very same street.

She determined to administer a gentle stimulant to the flagging spirits, and with a little preliminary cough to attract attention, she began—"I may as well inform you, young ladies, that I have been requested this year, as on previous occasions, to allow some of my young people, to attend in the ante-chamber of the assembly room with sandal ribbon, pins, and such little matter, and to be ready to repair any accidental injury to the ladies' dresses. I shall send four—of the most diligent." She laid a marked emphasis on the last words, but without much effect; they were too sleepy to care for any of the pomps and vanities, or, indeed, for any of the comforts of this world, excepting one sole things—their beds.

is mixed with agriculture, where the wife and daughters are at the needle . . . , while the men and the boys are at the plough." [23] Because there was a steady demand for gloves, this homemaker contributed regularly to the family's income. Jane Lewis tells about a Liverpool woman whose daughter remembered how her mother earned money. She reported:

> My Mam would buy sugar bags from the grocer's for a copper or so each. When she had a really big pile she would put two dolly tubs in the yard and fill one with red dye and one with blue and dye the bags. Then she'd make the blue into short pants and the red into dresses and sold them around the neighbourhood for between 9d. and ⅙ [about $1.50 to $2.50]. [24]

One man remembered wearing the blue pants as a child; he had hated them because they were scratchy and he had to keep them because they never wore out.

Dressmaking

A more sophisticated kind of piecework was dressmaking, one of the main occupations for women by the 1850s. Since making a dress was a large, complex project, often several women contributed to a single piece. One dressmaker was asked if she had sewn dresses by hand or on a machine when she was an apprentice. Her answer illustrates just how complex her job was:

Sewing machine. But more was done by hand then. All the finishing work was done by hand. There was a lot of hand-work and in those days linings were all tacked in and seamed in. We'd a lot of tacking and that carry-on to do. All skirts had braid and binding in them. Sometimes we'd four times to go round a skirt—the hem and then there was a binding. You ran that on all the way round the skirt and then turned it over to hem it in. That was three times round the skirt. Then they

This advertisement for a sewing machine depicts a team of dressmakers fitting a wealthy client for an elegant dress.

The Piecework Industry

❧

In *British Women in the Nineteenth Century*, Kathryn Gleadle explains how the piecework industry worked in Victorian England and the kinds of earnings women in this industry could expect.

In London a whole variety of trades proliferated, from the making of umbrellas, tennis balls and artificial flowers to the unpleasant grind of sack-stitching and of course, clothing. Many trades such as matchbox-making involved simple repetitive labour (in which children often assisted); but some of the domestic handicrafts involved a considerable degree of (unrecognised) skilled labour. A minority of women labouring in these industries might work in small workshops where they enjoyed the status and pay derived from making a product from start to finish. Most, however, were on piece rates, working in deskilled trades on a subcontracted basis. Wages for homework were chronically depressed and fell continually in value between 1870 and 1880, a factor which led to its reputation as "sweated" work. In the provinces remuneration was even worse than in the metropolis, with innovations such as the spread of the sewing machine from the 1850s failing to alter the status or pay of those engaged in clothing manufacture.

used to be six or seven yards wide a skirt, so you'd a bit of sewing to do.[25]

The availability of the cheap labor of apprentices, along with an abundance of mass-produced, high-quality fabrics available at a price that many middle-class women could afford, led to a rapid increase in the number of dressmakers. At the same time a growing number of newspapers carried advertisements of the latest fashions, increasing the demand for dresses. The combination of affordable fabrics and the desire to keep up with the latest fashion created the demand for dressmakers.

In 1842 London alone had fifteen thousand dressmakers and milliners; by 1863 there were seventeen thousand.

Apprentices in Dressmaking Shops

Sometimes an established dressmaker would begin receiving more orders than she could personally fill. When this happened, she would take on apprentices and turn a room in her house into a shop. Girls became apprentices in their teens for a period from five to seven years. Writers M. Phillips and W.S. Tomkinson explain how the apprentice system worked:

During this period she would work for her mistress, for the first few years for no wages at all, for the next few for a very small wage, in return for being taught the business. Sometimes she would sleep at the shop; almost always she would take her meals there. . . . At the end of her apprenticeship she would work for a few years for full wages and then, if she was a successful worker and had saved a little money, would set up in business on her own account and perhaps take apprentices herself. [26]

Working Conditions for Apprentices

Working conditions in dressmaking shops varied. A few shop owners took on only as many apprentices as they had room for, gave them decent food, and set reasonable working hours. Most of the shops, however, were crowded and dirty, and apprentices were forced to work up to eighteen hours per day. These were called sweatshops, and the apprentices were called sweated workers. The health of many girls working in sweatshops suffered under such conditions. A government report in 1842 noted that dressmaking produced more illness than any other occupation and presented more serious and frequently fatal problems. In 1843 a committee investigating working conditions in sweatshops interviewed doctors, who reported that workers suffered from headaches, indigestion, consumption (tuberculosis), and deteriorating eyesight. Assistant surgeon John Dalrymple saw a young woman who had come to the Royal London Ophthalmic Hospital for problems with her vision. He reported:

> Her working hours were eighteen in the day, occasionally even more; her meals, snatched with scarcely an interval or a few minutes from work, and her general health was evidently assuming a tendency to consumption. An appeal was made, by my directions, to her mistress for relaxation; but the reply was that in this last year of her apprenticeship her labours had become valuable, and that her mistress was entitled to them as recompense for teaching. [27]

Bad conditions continued in some dressmaking shops throughout the nineteenth century.

Despite its obvious drawbacks, dressmaking gave some women an opportunity to achieve a measure of financial independence. Many who established their shops as single women kept them after they married. They established prices and advertised, and they made out bills in their own names, not their husbands.' Besides allowing them to supplement the family earnings and also have their own savings, dressmaking afforded these women a measure of satisfaction in their own success.

Other Kinds of Piecework

Dresses were but one form of piecework. There were myriads of items that Victorian women made in their homes. Some piecework, such as footwear, hosiery, and lace, required machines, which women could rent. Makers of artificial flowers thrived because hats decorated with large, colorful flowers were fashionable. Eley explains, "English flowers have greatly improved during the last ten years [since 1865], consequently the demand for them has increased, and at the present time over seventy-five per cent of the flowers worn are English made."[28] One woman, who had the most unusual and most lucrative job of the pieceworkers, tied feathered flies and sold them to fishermen. Other women made cardboard boxes of all sizes, for which they had to supply their own glue and paste.

Retail Shopkeepers

Piecework was difficult and paid little. Still, it was considered a respectable way for a woman to contribute to the family's

An illustration shows two long lines of seamstresses at work on an assembly line in a dressmaking shop.

income. An equally respectable occupation was retail shop work. In *Penny Capitalists*, historian John Benson says, "Shopkeeping appeared to possess all that was lacking in other working-class jobs; comfort, security, independence and status."[29] Retail shops varied. Some were actual stores. For example, a Mrs. Cartwright operated a successful candy shop in a fashionable district. A Mrs. McGuire made pies in her kitchen and sold them. Most shops were small, like McGuire's, and sold a single type of merchandise, such as draperies, hats, shoes, crockery, or some food item.

Fly Tying as Piecework

In "How Women Earn a Living," published in a nineteenth-century issue of *Woman's Life,* an anonymous woman writer explains fly tying; the work she does as a successful pieceworker. Geoffrey Eley reprints her article in *The Ruined Maid: Modes and Manners of Victorian Women.*

I am a fisherman—or should I not rather say a fisherwoman—and therefore speak with authority when I say that fly tying is essentially a woman's work. Indeed as every fly fisher knows, the best flies are all tied by women, and, as these tyers are comparatively few, the price of high-class artificial flies continues enormously high. Amongst the best fly tyers known are Mrs. Ogden Smith and her daughter—now Mrs. Richardson—and it is needless to say that the orders daily pouring in on these ladies necessitates a large working staff.

Half-a-crown a dozen is the price paid for ordinary trout flies, and when we consider that a dozen are very quickly turned out by the adept, and that a single fisherman often orders as many as five or six dozen during the season, the income derived from such work can be very considerable.

This is realised when we remember that the stock-in-trade for such a business is practically *nil*. A single pair of scissors—by no means anything peculiar, and costing, say, half-a-crown—a pair of "fly tweezers" at two shillings, a small collection of various feathers, tiny fish hooks, and a reel of silk, are really all that is absolutely necessary. . . .

The most necessary feathers are those of the snipe and the jay's wing. These may be obtained from the poulterers at Leadenhall market, who make a point of saving such feathers for the fishermen's fly tyers, who often leave a standing order with such tradesmen for the special feathers they need.

By 1860 large stores selling a variety of goods, such as coats, children's clothing, curtains, carpets, and housewares, had evolved, and the term *department store* came into use. In these establishments, women, called shop assistants, waited on customers. With this development, in the space of four decades the number of women in the retail trades more than tripled from 87,000 in 1861 to 243,000 in 1901.

Working Conditions for Shop Assistants

Young women working as shop assistants endured difficult conditions and received low pay—usually two pence (about seventy-five cents) per hour. They worked seventy-five or more hours per week. They could take a total of forty-five minutes away from the counter to consume two meals, which were provided to them. They received about ten shillings per week (about twenty dollars), but they were required to live on or near the premises, and part of their salary went for room and board. Historian Kathryn Gleadle comments on the lodgings: "The larger shops often insisted that their junior staff live in lodgings provided by the firm. These were run on a profit-making basis and severely hampered the personal lives and freedom of the workforce."[30] This barrackslike housing was usually overcrowded, dirty, and had inadequate water and sanitation facilities. Women ate their meals of tea and bread in a damp basement. Moreover, shop assistants were closely supervised, and their pay could be docked for such offenses as giving the wrong change, tardiness, impoliteness to customers, or failing to make their beds in the barracks.

Shop assistants were expected to remain standing while on duty. After 1880 there was a movement to provide shop assistants with seats. An article published in 1880 in the *Englishwoman's Review* reports on a survey of shops aimed at discovering the extent to which owners were providing seats for shop assistants. Most of the milliners, bootmakers, and pub owners allowed women to sit down at intervals, but shops that had counters, such as drapers, china merchants, stationers, and bakers, provided no seats. Overall, only about one-fifth of the shop owners actually provided seats, and although some owners said the women were not forbidden to sit, many of these made no provisions for employees to do so.

Selling Services in Public Places

Women who worked in public accommodations, such as alehouses or inns, were also considered shopkeepers, and such occupations were considered appropriate for a woman. Conditions were often hard to endure, however. A barmaid gave an account of her work in a

Street vendors sell flowers and foodstuffs in this painting. Such jobs were not considered respectable for Victorian women.

letter to the editor of *Victoria Magazine* in June 1876:

> I live in a city house with six others, and we all work very hard, our hours being seventeen in a day. We open at 5.30 A.M., and close at 12.30 P.M. (midnight)....We are supposed to have two hours rest each a day, but this we only get three days out of six, and the other three days we have but an hour. We are supposed to be allowed to go out every third Sunday. Several of us have asked to be allowed to go out in rest time to get a breath of fresh air, but we have been refused for fear we should exceed our time. Therefore, from week's end to week's end, we have to inhale smoke, gas, and the foul breath of the numbers crowding at our bar, and we have no comfort, release, or relaxation from this dreary, wearing toil.[31]

Street Vendors

Less respected were street vendors. Button and lace hawkers were common. Others sold brushes and brooms, shoelaces, or stationery. Some were flower girls. In the essay "Street Traders," John Reynolds describes their work: "Flower girls—who tended to be very young, ragged, and barefoot—went to Covent Garden [an area in central London] early in the morning and made up bunches from flowers they bought or found discarded. Their profits might come to sixpence [about $2.25] a day." [32]

Most of the street traders sold food. Some women sold milk. Sometimes, husband-and-wife teams operated small, specialized food shops opening onto the street. The 1851 census listed 85,913 grocers, 14,320 greengrocers and fruiterers (those who sold only fresh vegetables and fruits), and 67,691 butchers. Women worked alongside their husbands, and if the man died, his widow usually continued to run the shop herself. Other women sold wares from booths at fairs and at weekly open-air markets. The largest markets took place on Saturday night and Sunday morning since working people usually received their week's pay on Saturday afternoon. Women prepared or purchased food to sell in their stalls: coffee, sandwiches, pea soup, fried fish, baked potatoes, pastries, sweets, hot cooked eels, meat pies, and luxuries such as pineapples and ices.

Most piecework and shop work required long hours, but the little money women brought in doing these jobs was important in supplementing family incomes. Still, these women could hardly be described as content with their lot in life. Historian David Rubinstein tells about a middle-class woman whose words express the difficulties of working women.

> Eleanor Marx, whose burdens were heavy and whose earnings were precarious, expressed what must have been a common view in a letter to her sister Laura Lafargue in 1889: "It's jolly hard though! I often think 'I'd rather be a kitten and cry mew' than a woman trying to earn a living." [33]

Chapter 3:
Women in a Life of Service

❧

Anearly endless progression of domestic duties describes the lives of most Victorian women. Some Victorian women, however—mostly girls, young women, and unmarried older women—worked as servants in the homes of others. A smaller number worked as governesses, nurses, midwives, or doctors. Like pieceworkers and shopkeepers, however, all of these women earned low pay for their hard work.

Domestic Service

With the growth of the middle class, increasing numbers of households employed one or more domestic servants. As a result, domestic service became the largest source of employment for women. During the middle and late Victorian period, about one-third of all working women between the ages of fifteen and twenty were employed as servants.

The nature of a servant's work depended on the social class of the employer: Middle-class families with lower incomes could afford no more than one servant, called the maid of all work; more-affluent middle-class families usually employed three servants, perhaps a kitchen servant, a governess, and a charwoman, who kept the house clean. Members of the upper class, with their large homes, employed large, structured staffs numbering up to forty servants.

A girl from a working-class family usually became a servant at age twelve or thirteen, working as a maid of all work. Going to work at such a young age could be wrenching. In 1875 Kate Faggetter, age twelve, wrote to her former headmistress: "I long to come home again to see some of my friends and playmates. . . . Dear Teacher we are having a new kitchen built and it does make me such a lot of work that I scarcely know how to do it."[34] She likely worked alone, was forbidden to have visitors, and slept on a thin mattress on the floor of the kitchen, which was located in the basement. These young servants were the first up in the morning and were on call until the mistress of the house went to bed, a workday of seventeen hours. A woman from Surrey remembered her first servant job in the home of a carpenter's family: "There was eleven children. . . . I didn't get no wages, only my food, one frock and one bonnet, and a shillin' to take home."[35]

Servants' Tasks

Domestic work was physically difficult and required knowledge of a wide variety of tasks. In an article entitled "Servants," Sally Mitchell lists the duties of a domestic in a middle-class household:

> Cooking, cleaning, sewing, washing, ironing, child care, filling and cleaning lamps, carrying coal and tending the open grates that heated individual rooms, hauling water up to bedrooms and slops down, going on errands, carrying parcels and luggage, walking the ladies of the household to social functions and waiting to accompany them home.[36]

Though women took pride in their role as servants, they were often overwhelmed by the amount of work.

In homes of wealthy Victorians with large domestic staffs, these tasks were delegated among the servants according to their rank. At the head of the female servants were the housekeeper and the head cook. The housekeeper was responsible for servants who worked in various parts of the house in clearly defined roles: the parlor maids, housemaids, nursery maids, and laundresses. The head cook was responsible for servants who had specialized tasks in the kitchen: the assistant cooks, kitchen maids, and scullery maids (dishwashers). Despite the limited nature

Most working-class Victorian women were employed as domestic servants like the one in this painting.

of their jobs, servants in large houses had to rise early to complete them. One woman recalled that she got up at 4 A.M. every morning to bake fresh bread and churn butter for the breakfast of her mistress, Lady Wilbraham. Housemaids also had to rise at 4 A.M. to finish the cleaning before the family came downstairs. Any servant seen by a member of the family with a duster in her hand was dismissed immediately.

All of the servants took their meals and socialized in the basement. At the end of the day, servants used the enclosed back stairs to reach their sleeping rooms, which were located in the attic. During the day, servants used the back stairs to carry clean water to the family's quarters and carry the slops and chamber pots back down. Using the back stairs kept servants and their work out of the family's sight and reinforced distinctions between social classes.

A Day Cleaning Girl

Most young girls worked as servants and lived with their employers. A few worked as day cleaning girls, called charwomen as adults, like a Mrs. Wilkinson, who recalls her first job as a daily cleaner. Her story is retold in *A Woman's Place* by Elizabeth Roberts.

I went as a day cleaning girl for twelve months. I was fourteen on the 5th August and a friend of our Edith's came down to see if I'd take her job over as a morning girl for Mrs. Postlethwaite which m'mother said, "Take." I was only about fourteen and six days and I took the job and it was only three-and-six a week but I only worked mornings. . . . I used to do vegetables, and the rough cleaning. There was no hoover. . . . I'd to brush the carpets, and I'd to take the stair carpet on the lawn and drag it up and down the lawn. It was hard work for a girl of fourteen, and I didn't like it. . . . But I'd to stand outside on the bay window and all those tiny little windows I'd to clean every one of them with pan shine about once a month. It was pretty hard work. Anyway I was there until I was fifteen and a half. Oh, I came home, and I'd to chop firewood of course and I'd chop m'fingers. M'father used to say, "Bring it home and I'll chop it." I'd chopped m'finger, and m'hands were chapped with cleaning those outsides, it was frosty weather. Oh, I was generally fed up. My hands were sore and I was tired and I probably didn't like the job anymore but I always liked Miss Postlethwaite, she was always very nice.

The Difficulties of Cleaning and Washing

No matter who ended up doing it, housework was time-consuming and difficult. In an age before specialized cleaning agents had been developed, people had to make their own cleaning supplies, using recipes gleaned from books and magazines. For example, in the essay "Housework and Domestic Technology," Julia M. Gergits explains, "Potatoes smashed into a pulp and mixed with water were used to clean curtains; vitriol (a mild form of sulfuric acid) and lemon juice removed stains from marble."[37] Individual fireplaces, the main source of heat, had to be swept and the iron grates had to be cleaned, polished, and restocked with coal before the room was cleaned. Vacuum cleaners had yet to be invented, so servants swept rugs, took them outdoors, and beat them to remove the ground-in dust.

An especially difficult chore was washing clothes. Washing machines would not be developed until the early 1900s, so all the clothes and household linens had to be washed by hand. Before the washing even began, servants carried in water from an outdoor tap, usually the night before wash day, and then they rose at 2 A.M. to heat it in a boiler over a fire. Perkin gives the details:

Clothes were put in to soak the evening prior to washday, and the next morning put in hot water in a tub, then rotated by hand with a dolly [a wooden implement with three legs and a stout handle]. The clothes were rubbed where necessary, boiled for half an hour, rinsed, blued [rinsed in blue-colored water to make white clothes whiter] and starched. This process was repeated for different kinds of clothes and household linens, "whites" coming first, "coloureds" next and heavily soiled clothes last of all.[38]

It took major physical effort to wring out sheets and other heavy items. In wealthy homes a team of servants would work at this task, but in less-affluent homes this chore would fall to a single servant.

Low Status and Poor Pay

Despite working so hard, domestic servants were given little respect. Employers demanded subservient behavior, requiring servants to stay out of sight or to stand if they had to be in the presence of their employers. In his essay "Domestic Service and Democracy," Victorian social critic Edward Salmon noted that "the barrier between the drawing-room and the servants' hall is never passed. Life above the stairs is as entirely severed from life below stairs as is the life of one house from another."[39] Nor did servants have the respect of the community at large. One young servant dreaded scrubbing the front

In this painting, a servant tends to her lady's needs as she dresses for the day.

step because passersby jeered at her. Worse still, perhaps, servants could not expect any consideration from their employers. For example, Rose Ashton had just finished cleaning up after Christmas dinner when her mistress sent her to the toilet with string, a big needle, and a heap of papers to make toilet paper.

> I sat there on Christmas Day and I think I cried a bucketful of tears. Christmas afternoon and I was ... sit-

ting cutting bits of paper, bits of paper like that and getting this big needle, threading them and tying knots in them and tying them on these hoops, till about half past four when I went in for m'tea. Sitting there on the lavatory seat. [40]

Middle-Class Women Worked as Governesses

Whereas society considered servant work suitable for working-class girls and women, society disapproved of middle-class girls and women taking those jobs since the expectation was that they would marry a man with the means to support them and uphold middle-class values. Some middle-class girls and women did have to work if their fathers or husbands died. Other women could not find husbands since in Victorian England there were fewer men than women. For these women, one job available to them was the position of governess. A governess taught well-off middle- and upper-class children; ordinarily she lived with the family. The qualifications of a governess made her something of a contradiction in terms—a fact Victorians understood. In an article published in the *Quarterly Review* in December 1848, writer and reformer Elizabeth Eastlake defines a governess:

> The real definition of a governess, in the English sense, is a being who is

Working-Class Homes

Working-class homes were simple and sparsely furnished; nevertheless, homemakers prided themselves in having a clean house and at least one pretty item. A Mrs. Mitchell recalls washing and ironing special curtains. Her story is retold in *A Woman's Place* by Elizabeth Roberts.

vie with each other, who could have the nicest curtains. Of course, some didn't bother, they did any old rag up. But I remember coming home and thinking Mummy's put up clean curtains, they used to look so lovely.

Even in working-class homes, Victorian women took special care of treasured items.

Turn it [the wringer] with one hand and guide the clothes through with the other. That was the washing. Well, there was all the ironing. Now in those days, we had Nottingham lace curtains, they were full-length, beautiful lace, and the ends were scalloped. Almost everyone had these. Now all those had to be washed by hand, and then they were all starched and we used to have to get hold, the children, mother would work one end and the children at the other, and we pulled them like this, draw them together and pull and that was to straighten them and then all that had to be ironed and it was who could have the nicest curtains. They were really houseproud, you know. They used to our equal in birth, manners, and education, but our inferior in worldly wealth. Take a lady, in every meaning of the word, born and bred, and let her father pass through the gazette [bankruptcy], and she wants nothing more to suit our highest *beau ideal* [model] of a guide and instructress to our children. [41]

A woman might became a governess if she had no father, brother, or husband to provide her with financial support.

The governess's duties varied depending on the family with whom she lived. In her primary role, she taught the girls in the family (the boys were tutored or sent away to school) all of their subjects, which included English, arithmetic, drawing, sketching, painting, music, French (perhaps Latin and German, too), history, geography, and needlework. Just how much a girl tutored this way might have learned would likely have varied. Since no higher education was available for women, few governesses would have mastered even a few of these subjects. In some families, such as the home of writer William Thackeray, the governess took the girls shopping, read aloud to them while they embroidered, and generally supervised them. In Yorkshire in 1850, Jane Ellen Harrison said that her governess taught her to memorize facts and poetry, "how to enter a room, how to get into a carriage, that little girls should be seen and not heard, and that I was in the schoolroom to learn, not to ask questions." [42]

A Lack of Identity and Freedom

Governesses often found themselves in a position that was socially ambiguous. In the essay "On Governesses," published in 1848, Lady Eastlake says:

We shall ever prefer to place those immediately about our children who have been born and bred with somewhat of the same refinement as ourselves. We must ever keep them in a sort of isolation, for it is the only means for maintaining that distance which the reserve of English manners and the decorum of English families exact [demand]. [43]

In addition to the lack of clear definition of her place in society, a governess lacked any kind of personal freedom. Governesses worked all day, giving children their baths and meals as well as their lessons; they did mending for the family and shared a bedroom with the children and sometimes even a bed at night. Victorian novelist Charlotte Brontë, who worked as a governess of the children of a wealthy householder, wrote to her sister, "She [Mrs. Sidgwick] cares nothing about me, except to contrive how the greatest possible quantity of labour may be got out of me;

In this English painting, a governess sits forlorn and isolated as the girls she tutors enjoy leisure time.

and to that end she overwhelms me with oceans of needlework, yards of cambric to hem, muslin nightcaps to make, and, above all things, dolls to dress." [44]

A Lack of Respect

Adding to the governess's trials was the fact that the children often reflected the attitudes of their parents. As a consequence, they were often disobedient, taunting, and cruel. Such behavior, in turn, tended to bring out the worst in governesses; some governesses were disrespectful of their charges, to the chil-

dren's detriment. Mary Gladstone, wife of a British political leader, recalled, "My governess from ten to seventeen years continued to treat me as half-witted, so I grew up a nonentity. I have never outgrown it." [45] With all the difficult conditions, some governesses, however, developed warm relations with the children. Sybil Cuffe had a governess she loved, "an excellent teacher who 'made no attempt to invade our emotional life, and was kind, just and reserved.'" [46]

Like other Victorian working women, governesses received low pay. They received

Charlotte Brontë's Work as a Governess

In *English Women in Life and Letters,* M. Phillips and W.S. Tomkinson reprint a July 1839 letter from novelist Charlotte Brontë to her friend; in the letter, she describes her experiences as a governess. Brontë did not want to be a governess, but she took the job out of duty.

I cannot procure ink without going into the drawing-room, where I do not wish to go. If you were near me, perhaps I might be tempted to tell you all, and to pour out the long history of a private governess's trials and crosses in her first situation. As it is I will only ask you to imagine the miseries of a reserved wretch like me, thrown at once into the midst of a large family at a time when the house was filled with company—people whose faces I had never seen before. In this state I had charge given me of a set of pampered, spoilt, turbulent children whom I was expected constantly to amuse, as well as to instruct. I soon found that the constant demand on my stock of animal spirits reduced them to the lowest state of exhaustion; at times I felt and, I suppose, seemed—depressed. To my astonishment I was taken to task on the subject by Mrs.———with a sternness of manner and a harshness of language scarcely credible; like a fool, I cried most bitterly. I thought I had done my best—strained every nerve to please her; and to be treated in that way, merely because I was shy and sometimes melancholy, was too bad. Mrs.———behaves somewhat more civilly to me now than she did at first, and the children are a little more manageable; but she does not know my character, and she does not wish to know it. I have never had five minutes' conversation with her since I came, except while she was scolding me.

room and board but no compensation to cover clothing, laundry, travel, and medical care. Salaries ranged from fifteen to a hundred pounds (about six hundred to four thousand dollars) a year, about equal to what a housekeeper or cook earned. Most governesses got along on twenty to thirty pounds (eight hundred to twelve hundred dollars) a year.

By the end of the nineteenth century, the job of governess was almost entirely phased out. Laws had been passed requiring communities to establish schools for girls, and women who would otherwise have worked as governesses became teachers instead.

Early-Nineteenth-Century Nursing

Just as the job of governess evolved over the course of the Victorian era, so too did jobs in the health professions. In the early years of the century, nurses had no training. Some of them were village women who had taken care of their own children and sick relatives. A woman named Mrs. Scott, who lived in north Yorkshire, was this kind of untrained nurse. Her granddaughter remembered that she attended at every birth in the parish, and "when the children wasn't well, people used to send 'em to Granny's; 'Mam's sent me to see what you think *this* spot is.' . . . She was very clever with herbal remedies."[47] Other nurses worked in public hospitals for about one shilling a day. They did everything for patients assigned to their care, sleeping on a cot beside the patient, preparing all the meals, and providing personal care. Nurses during these early years of the nineteenth century had poor reputations. A nurse's patients were more likely to die than recover, although this had as much to do with the poor sanitation in the hospital as it did with any action by the nurse. Moreover, nurses who went to the homes of sick people were reputed to steal from their patients and drink on the job. Florence Nightingale, whose later crusading led to enormous improvements in the training of nurses, said that nursing was done by those "who were too old, too weak, too drunken, too dirty, too stolid, or too bad to do anything else."[48]

The Influence of Florence Nightingale

Florence Nightingale eventually became a strong advocate for improving the status of nurses. In 1861 she used funds donated in her honor to open a nursing school at St. Thomas's Hospital. In training nurses, she taught new techniques in

Florence Nightingale tends to the needs of wounded English soldiers in Turkey during the Crimean War.

cleanliness and patient care. She urged young women to train for the nursing profession, but she also lobbied hard for better pay for nurses. In the June 1876 issue of *Victoria Magazine,* she said,

> A young woman who has to work must begin before 25; a nurse's life is so arduous that the usual computation allows them 12 years of work, after which time they are incapacitated. Is it a career likely to tempt a woman of culture, to commence at 25 upon wages which an incompetent servant maid of 18 refuses? . . . Surely a well-trained sick nurse—when we consider all the needful qualifications—is worth more than a kitchen maid. [49]

At the same time that Nightingale was developing training institutions for nurses, large cities were demanding more nurses because the population was rising. To meet this demand, Queen Victoria agreed to spend seventy thousand pounds to establish district nursing services to train nurses to fill the new posts. In the cities, nurses worked in large hospitals. The queen's nurses also worked as village nurses. After training, a village nurse worked from a home base provided for her. She could act as a midwife; care for wounds; and administer medicines, such as quinine, linseed, and cod-liver oil, which she supplemented with gin, brandy, port,

eggs, and tea. An inspector wrote in his July 1892 report about a woman, known only as Nurse Egan: "Once a week she goes to the Lady Manager [of her region] who hears from her about her cases. . . . Nurse Egan has been supplied with a donkey cart to help her in the great distances she has to go." [50]

Victorian Women as Midwives

Midwifery was a separate service provided by women, but it often overlapped with nursing. Poor women hired midwives to deliver their babies because their fees for attending a birth were just a few shillings (between eight and twelve dollars in 1881). Doctors charged much more than poor women could afford. A midwife's fee included delivering the baby and bathing and dressing it. The fee also included a return every day for four days and every other day for four more days to care for the infant.

Many poor women trusted the midwives, who had learned their skills from experience. Social historian Mary Chamberlain noted their success and that "[the midwife] was more patient [than doctors] in her attendance. She was also less likely to interfere; midwives did not use instruments and rarely inserted their hand inside a labouring woman unlike many of the doctors. . . . The naturalness of her technique often meant fewer complications." [51]

Women Medical Students

In *Victorian Feminism, 1850–1900,* Philippe Levine quotes nurse Florence Nightingale's views regarding women who wanted to become doctors. Men who hoped to protect the medical profession for themselves, urged women to become nurses instead.

Ladies who desire to study and practise medicine are told that it is unfeminine and unladylike, besides being too laborious for their sex, and are urged instead to become nurses. . . . The strains upon the nerves and physical strength, the violence done to delicacy, the necessity of witnessing painful and disgusting sights, are greater in the case of the nurse . . . while many of the offices that have to be performed by her, are in themselves of so repulsive a character to anyone not bred to menial service, that only strong affection or enthusiasm could overcome the disgust attending them; but then, neither high pay nor social position are to be attained by the nurse, while both are claimed by the physician. It has, therefore, been decided that it is highly unfeminine, nay, revolting to every feeling of womanly delicacy, for a woman to be a physician, but most feminine to be a nurse.

Early in the Victorian era, women usually worked as midwives without formal training. In the 1830s the maternity hospital known as the British Ladies Lying In Institution trained a few women as midwives. By 1872 the Obstetrical Society, an organization of doctors who specialized in obstetrics, had set up a three-month training course for midwives and registered those who took the course and passed the exam. Some doctors also helped women become midwives on an informal basis. Mrs. Layton, who wanted training but could not afford the fees charged for the course by the Obstetrical Society, worked with doctors more or less as an apprentice. She would ask them questions and read reference books on her own. "There were three doctors who were very good to me and were willing to lend me books or to teach me anything. I was taught to deliver with forceps, which midwives are not taught in hospitals."[52]

Women Struggle to Become Doctors

Women might become skilled midwives, but until 1850 none had become doctors. Eventually, women were allowed to study medicine, although they encountered obstacles that required patience, endurance, and determination to overcome. Men who controlled admission to medical school did not want women to be enrolled, and although they could not refuse to let women enroll when they scored high marks on the entrance exams, they did not go out of their way to welcome them. If a woman succeeded in obtaining admission to medical school, she was taunted and abused by her classmates, especially if she scored high marks. At first, women who completed classes would find that they were not given credit for having done so. Once women overcame that obstacle, they were given a certificate of completion, but not a regular medical degree. Later, when women had succeeded in obtaining regular medical degrees, they were barred from medical societies, which were responsible for keeping doctors up to date in their profession.

In the face of such obstacles, some women went abroad to study. For example, Elizabeth Garrett Anderson, after experiencing extreme resistance in her efforts to obtain a medical education in Britain, went to the University of the Sorbonne in Paris. There she was admitted, took both her written and oral exams in French, and received her doctor of medicine degree in 1870. In 1872 she developed London's New Hospital for Women and Children and in 1874 helped to establish the London Medical College for Women, where she then taught for twenty-three years. Despite her obvious competence,

when she married and had children, fellow doctors tried to force her to give up her medical work and stay home.

Even when women finally were admitted to British medical schools, they faced extreme hostility from fellow students. The experience of Sophia Jex-Blake and four other women who were allowed to study medicine at the University of Edinburgh in Scotland in 1869 was typical. The five women were serious, hardworking students and earned a number of honors and prizes. As the women left the building after the award ceremony, male students, angry that women had received prizes, started to riot. Editors Carol Bauer and Lawrence Ritt explain the outcome:

> They were protected, however, by a small number of sympathetic male students, who formed an escort for the beleaguered women. Even after the riot had subsided they had to contend with threats of physical violence, hisses, shouts of "whore," and jibes that "they'd never do it [go to medical school] if they could get married."[53]

Victorian women employed in service jobs struggled, whether as domestic servants, governesses, teachers, nurses, midwives, or doctors. They most often worked hard for low pay and sometimes had to fight societal customs and prejudice. Their hard work, however, led to improved conditions for other women in the future.

Chapter 4:
Women Employed in Industry

Women who worked in industry most visibly departed from the Victorian middle-class ideal of wife, mother, and homemaker. Pieceworkers and shopkeepers could attain some of that ideal by working in the home or by dressing glamorously in a shop. Servants and governesses worked for a family and lived in a home doing tasks of child care and homemaking. Women working in these roles attained an element of respectability, even if only in their own minds. Those who took jobs on farms, in factories, or in mines, however, could make no such claim. For them, the Victorian ideal was virtually unachievable.

Women Hired by Their Husbands' Employers

The Victorian era was a time when farms were more and more owned by wealthy landholders who hired men on a temporary basis to do planting and harvesting of crops. These landholders made it a condition of employment that their workers' wives could also be called upon to help during busy times. Social historian Pamela Horn explains, "Newspaper advertisements for labourers in Dorset often referred to the need for the successful candidate to have a 'working family.' And in the late 1860s there were reports of wives in that county having to send a daughter or another substitute because they were unable to work themselves."[54] One laborer's wife, known only as Mrs. Grout, complained that she had to take her six children into the field with her when the landowner asked her to help on his farm, where he grew hops and turnips, among other crops. She began her work in the spring picking stones and preparing the ground for sowing. She explained the tasks for the year:

Then in May and June hop-tying; last year me and another took 10 acres at 4s. [about $8.00] an acre, two poles to the stock [every stalk of the plant was supported by and tied to two poles]; we usually only get 3s. [about $6.00] or 3s. 6d. [$7.00] an acre. It takes all a woman's time to tie five acres; children

Two farmwives deposit sheaves of harvested grain in this painting.

and tailing turnips at 7s. [about $14.00] an acre. [55]

Some farmers allowed laborers to plant potatoes in their fields for the personal use of the laborers' families. The customary payment for this privilege was free labor from the laborers' wives.

Women Did Hard Physical Work

Not all women worked as part of their husbands' obligations. Records of farm wages indicate that some women did the farmwork on their own and were paid for it. For example, four women working at a farm called Ireley worked between 100 and 150 days a year. They carried out the difficult work of "threshing, stone-picking, dung spreading, weeding, hoeing, sorting and planting potatoes, fruit picking, haymaking and harvesting, work in the garden, household chores and mending sacks." [56] The most active of the four, Emma Seabright, who had three children, earned five pounds, fifty-two pence (about $220) for the year.

Many women prided themselves in being able to do the same work as men even though they were paid about half as much. Of the tasks, reaping with a sickle was among the hardest. In *Toilers of the Field,* published in 1892, author Richard Jefferies described women working as reapers:

cannot help at that. Then from June to August haymaking and harvest. . . . In September hopping [gathering hops, a twining vine whose dried flowers are used in making beer], at which I can earn 1s. 2d. [about $2.50] a day; . . . then comes fruit-picking at 8d. [about $1.40] a day and cider; and last topping

From earliest dawn to latest night they swing the sickles, staying with their husbands, and brothers, and friends. . . . Grasping the straw continuously cuts and wounds the hand, and even gloves will hardly give perfect protection. The woman's bare neck is turned to the colour of tan; her thin muscular arms a bronze right up to the shoulder. Short time is allowed for refreshment; right through the hottest part of the day they labour. It is remarkable that . . . very few cases of sunstroke occur. [57]

After the harvest, many women, who had worked all day, returned to the fields in the evening for gleaning. They walked the fields, carrying a sack, and picked up the scattered grain left behind by the harvesters. This practice, permitted by the owner, was a source of grain that the women ground into flour for their own use.

Women as Migrant Workers

Another form of agricultural labor for women was migrant work. Almost every county in England had a special crop that needed to be harvested by an influx of workers at a particular time in the year. For example, in April and May, Worchestershire needed workers to strip the bark from willow branches, which would then be woven into baskets; Gilford need-

ed workers to wash carrots in the winter; and Carshaltom needed workers as transplanters in the spring and vegetable harvesters in the fall. When landholders could not find a sufficient supply of workers locally, they hired migrant workers. They paid commissions to agencies that organized workers and made them available to farmers.

A hardy peasant girl poses with her sickle before the harvest.

Life for all migrant workers was hard. They had to travel on their own to the locations where agents were hiring. Women walked from as far away as west Wales, distances as long as forty miles, telling stories, singing, and even knitting as they walked. Landholders who hired migrants every year provided minimal facilities where workers slept and ate. For example, at a farm called Dippenhall, the

Four Years in an Agriculture Gang

In *Strong-Minded Women and Other Lost Voices from the Nineteenth Century,* Janet Horowitz Murray reprints an excerpt from *Life as We Have Known It* by a Mrs. Burrows. Burrows recalls the kind gesture of a shepherd's wife on a cold day when she was a gang worker.

In all the four years I worked in the fields, I never worked one hour under cover of a barn, and only once did we have a meal in a house. And I shall never forget that one meal or the woman who gave us it. It was a most terrible day. The cold east wind (I suppose it was an east wind, for surely no wind ever blew colder), and the sleet and snow which came every now and then in showers seemed almost to cut us to pieces. We were working upon a large farm that lay halfway between Croyland and Peterborough. Had the snow and sleet come continuously we should have been allowed to come home, but because it only came at intervals, of course we had to stay. . . . Dinner-time came, and we were preparing to sit down under a hedge and eat our cold dinner and drink our cold tea, when we saw the shepherd's wife coming towards us, and she said to the ganger, "Bring these children into my house and let them eat their dinner there." We went into that very small two-roomed cottage, and when we got into the largest room there was not standing room for us all, but this woman's heart was large, even if her house was small, and so she put here few chairs and table out into the garden, and then we all sat down in a ring upon the floor. She then placed in our midst a very large saucepan of hot boiled potatoes, and bade us help ourselves. Truly, although I have attended scores of grand parties and banquets since that time, not one of them has seemed half as good to me as that meal did. . . .

For four years, summer and winter, I worked in these gangs—no holidays of any sort, with the exception of very wet days and Sundays—and at the end of that time it felt like Heaven to me when I was taken to the town of Leeds, and put to work in a factory.

Women of Victorian England

A painting depicts a group of women gleaning scattered grain left behind by the harvesters.

owner, Mrs. Paine, had two hundred acres of hops. In 1868 she needed 2,660 workers, which agents supplied. Paine provided food and accommodations:

> Migrant pickers were housed in large sheds, sleeping on beds of straw. Mrs. Paine supplied a pair of sheets and a counterpane [quilt] for each bed, but there were no proper washing or sanitary facilities, and no means of drying wet clothes, other than the camp fires on which pickers cooked their meals. Bread, tea and herrings were the most popular items of food among the Dippenhall workers.[58]

Women in Agriculture Gangs

While individual migrant workers traveled long distances to the locations of employment, agriculture gangs operated as a unit, moving from farm to farm in their local areas. Gangs operated in the east and north of England, where fewer people lived and where farms tended to be smaller. Gang members, who either were girls too young to be away from home for a season or mothers who needed to stay with their families, went home every night. They worked by the day under the supervision of a gang master, who had contracted with a local farmer to bring in workers. At the height of the gang system, about six thousand people—more than half of them women and girls and many of them children as young as five—worked in gangs. Women earned three or four pence (about $1.00 or $1.25) a day and the children one or two pence. Gangs cut and hauled hay, worked at grain harvest, peeled osier (willow twigs for baskets), picked peas, gathered potatoes, and pulled turnips.

Many of the women were recruited through local hiring fairs. Diarist Arthur Munby records his observations of a hiring fair on a visit to York, where he saw "a double row of farm lasses, standing for hire on the pavement: They were homely wenches, . . . plainly drest, some wearing cotton gloves. . . . [The girls were] honest and stolid looking creatures." [59] Once hired, young women walked, sometimes up to five miles, to the place where the gang was scheduled to work.

Woman gang workers had the hardest role of all agriculture workers. They put in long hours, did heavy physical work, and endured cruelty from gang masters. Because gangs operated in the north and the east, where the weather is colder and rainier, many workers became sick or were injured by working in bad weather conditions. In an interview with a representative from the Government Employment Commission, eighteen-year-old Mary Ann Gallay from Norfolk reported that she worked in a gang of thirty-seven people from 8 A.M. until 6 P.M. in summer and to 3 P.M. in winter. She worked in rain in summer, and in winter she handled icy vegetable roots until her hands became chapped and painful.

Sarah Ann Roberts, also of Norfolk, was permanently injured as a result of weeding grain for days in the damp weather, and she received no medical help or compensation. She reported:

> I have been so wet that I have taken off my clothes and wrung them out and hung them up to dry on the top of the wheat . . . while we went in again to weed. . . . We have had to take off our shoes and pour the water out, and then the man [gang master] would say, "Now then, go in again." . . . My knee is so bad, and nearly as big as that loaf [of bread], but I have to keep moving with a crutch and stick. . . . The man knocked us about and ill-used us dreadfully with hoes, spuds [spades], and everything. [60]

Opposition to Agriculture Gangs

The opponents of the gang system, however, were not as critical of the conditions under which women worked as they were about the moral hazards of the job. Girls, they suspected, learned and used bad language in gangs and failed to be educated in proper feminine graces. Others were concerned about mixed gangs since some girls had been seduced by gang masters or male fellow workers. Most of the trouble occurred on the long walk home after work rather than on the job.

The number of women employed in agriculture gradually declined. The Gang Act of 1867 prohibited children under age eight from working in gangs, limited the distance workers had to walk to work, and provided women with female supervisors. The Education Act of 1876 required children to go to school and restricted children younger than ten from gang work.

Gradually, during the last quarter of the century, men's wages improved, and as a result many wives and daughters no longer needed to work in the gangs. The acts of 1867 and 1876, however, did not directly affect migrant workers. The number of migrant workers decreased because machines took over many of the jobs formerly done by hand. Women who were displaced by machines moved to the cities and found work in factories.

Women as Factory Workers

As women gradually played less of a role in agricultural work, they played an increasing role in manufacturing. With

---

A Hiring Fair

❧

Some rural towns held hiring fairs twice a year for farm employers to find either indoor or outdoor workers. Those who were looking for work stood in a specified area until a farmer approached and they agreed to a six-month term. Workers received room and board but no wages until the end of the six months, a practice designed to prevent the worker from quitting. In *A Woman's Place,* Elizabeth Roberts records a Mrs. Armstrong's memory of one hiring fair.

We went to farm service and we used to walk from here to Ulverston,

wait till eleven o'clock till they started. The old farmers used to come up King Street and say, "Is tha for hiring lass?" I used to say, "Aye." He'd say, "What's tha asking?" We used to say, "What are you going to give us?" "I'll give you four pound ten." We'd say, "No thank you." We used to walk on a bit farther down King Street and another farmer would come up and say, "Is tha for hiring lass." Perhaps we'd get five pound ten off him for the six month. He used to say, "Can you wash, can you bake, can you scrub?"

the development of steam-driven machines, large numbers of workers were needed to control such devices as spinning machines and enormous looms. The textile industry was dominant in Victorian England, with cotton factories outnumbering the combined number of wool, linen, and silk factories. By 1851 textile factories in England employed about 385,000 women. The textile industry employed women generally in three kinds of jobs: preparing raw material, such as cotton or wool; spinning the raw material into thread; and weaving the thread into cloth. Spinning required two workers—a slubber, whose job was to twist the raw material, and a spinner to run the machine. Children were employed to remove bobbins when they were full of thread and replace them with empty ones.

Women, who composed the largest number of textile workers, worked in difficult conditions. At work they sat in large rooms full of machines and did the same monotonous tasks over and over. In *Victorian People and Ideas,* Richard D. Altick describes the workers' conditions before Parliament passed protective laws:

They were deafened by the noise of the steam engines and the clattering machinery and stifled in air that not only was laden with dust but, in the absence of ventilation, was heated to as high as eighty-five degrees. The workers were driven to maximum output by strict overseers, fined for spoiling goods, dozing off, looking out the window, and other derelictions, and forever imperiled by unguarded shafts, belts, and flywheels. Industrial diseases and those caused simply by the proximity of many unwashed, chronically ill human bodies conspired with accidents to disable and kill them. [61]

A woman named Alice Foley, who had worked in the factory as a girl, remembered the noise, dirt, and heat. She said, "At first I was highly terrified by the noise and the proximity of clashing machinery." [62] In 1852 76 percent of employed fourteen-year-old girls were factory workers.

There were other factories besides the textile mills. In match factories, for example, women made matches and girls packed them. These factories reportedly had some of the worst conditions. Phosphorus, an ingredient used in making matches, damaged workers' jaws and teeth, a condition that occurred because women held match sticks in their teeth. Matchboxes were filled by girls who were paid by the piece for taking matches out of frames and putting them into boxes. In the essay "The 'White Slavery' of London Match Workers," published in 1888, writer Annie Besant explains:

About three frames can be done in an hour, and ½d. [about nine cents]

This English drawing shows women and girls working in a match factory, where working conditions were abysmal.

is paid for each frame emptied; only one frame is given out at a time, and the girls have to run downstairs and upstairs each time to fetch the frame, thus much increasing their fatigue. One of the delights of the frame work is the accidental firing of the matches; when this happens the worker loses the work, and if the frame is injured she is fined or "sacked."[63]

Bad Conditions Lead to Government Acts

Women and young girls worked long hours in the factories for little pay. For example, Elizabeth Bentley, who was twenty-three in 1832, told a parliamentary committee investigating working hours for women and children that she had started working in a linen factory when she was six years old. "She worked as a 'little doffer' (taking full bobins off spinning frames and replacing them) from six in the morning until seven at night in the slow season, and from five in the morning until nine at night in the six months of the year when the mill was busy."[64]

Parliament eventually passed laws that limited the hours that women and children could be forced to work. In 1833 an act prohibited the employment of girls under the age of nine and limited the work of girls under twelve to forty-eight hours a week. The 1847 act restricted the employment of women and children to ten hours a day. Yet some abuses continued. A factory inspector, testifying in Parliament, said that factory owners liked to employ women for long day shifts and night work because they could pay women less than men and more easily persuade women to continue working even when they were exhausted. An 1883 survey of over seventeen thousand female factory workers indicated that a woman averaged the equivalent of $3.37 per week and a man averaged $8.26.

Children Suffered from Neglect and Poverty

Joseph Corbett, who lived during the Victorian era, recalls how his family was affected by his mother's long work hours in a factory. Despite her hard work, the family still lived in poverty. His story is reprinted in *English Women in Life and Letters* by M. Phillips and W.S. Tomkinson.

My mother worked in a manufactory from a very early age. She was clever and industrious, and moreover she had a reputation of being virtuous. She was regarded as an excellent match for a working man. She married early—she became the mother of eleven children; I am the eldest. To the best of her ability she performed the important duties of a wife and mother. She was lamentably deficient in domestic knowledge, in that most important of all human instruction, how to make the home and fireside possess a charm for her husband and children, she had never received one single lesson. As the family increased, so anything like comfort disappeared altogether. She made many efforts to abstain from shop work; but her pecuniary necessities [money problems] forced her back into the shop. The family was large, and every moment was required at home. I have known her, after the close of a hard day's work, [to] sit up nearly all night for several nights together washing and mending of clothes. My father could have no comfort here, and he from an ignorant mistaken notion sought comfort in the alehouse.

My mother's ignorance of household duties; my father's consequent irritability and intemperance; the frightful poverty; the constant quarreling; the pernicious example to my brothers and sisters; the bad effect upon the future conduct of my brothers, one and all of us being forced out to work so young that our feeble earnings would only produce 1 s a week; cold and hunger; and the innumerable sufferings of my childhood, crowd upon my mind and overpower me.

Issues Relating to Child Care and Homemaking

Women working long hours in factories for low pay raised public concern about child care and homemaking. In 1894 Mrs. Ashworth from Burnley, Lancashire, conducted a survey of the conditions of children when their mothers went to the mill every day. The primary concern was that children were being left unattended, although the results suggested that this was less a problem than she had anticipated. "Out of 160 cases she investigated, half the children were left with relatives, nearly half with neighbours; only in nine cases were children left with no one to take care of them." [65] Still, a debate continued about the causes and prevention of infant death and the concern that pregnant women working in factories had to stand for many hours a day. Many women worked right up to the time of birth. Some women even had their babies while at their looms.

The issue of homemaking drew a mixture of opinions. Politician Anthony Ashley Cooper, arguing in 1844 for the ten-hour day on the floor of Parliament, said,

Everything runs to waste; the wife can do nothing for her husband and family; she can neither cook, wash, repair clothes, or take charge of the infants; all must be paid for out of her scanty earnings, and after all, most imperfectly done. Dirt, discomfort, ignorance, recklessness, are the portion of such households; the wife has no time for learning in her youth, and none for practice in her riper age. [66]

On the other hand, another observer disagreed with this assessment, stating that women had no more time for housekeeping when they worked at home.

In fact, married women factory workers tended to be well organized and good managers. From the earliest days, for instance, Lancashire women cotton workers arranged their own networks of support, using friends, relatives, old people and young girls between seven and eleven to help with housework, washing, [and] child-minding. [67]

Whatever its disadvantages, some women liked factory work. It was warmer in a factory than outside in a field and was less isolated than servant work. Many women liked the friendly interchange with fellow workers. Girls living at home with their parents could often save money for a wedding, and married women could often save a little to spend on themselves. One woman, after sixty years of factory life, said that whatever she earned herself was worth twice as much as whatever her husband gave her. She liked the feeling of independence and the opportunity to earn enough money to pay for a night out.

Women as Miners

If at least a few women found factory work rewarding, the same could hardly be said of mining. In 1841 seven thousand women and girls worked in mines and quarries, over two thousand of them in coal mines. In some parts of Britain, such as Pembrokeshire in western Wales, where there was no other work for them, women made up 30 percent of mine workers. This was underground work, a dangerous occupation that had the worst accident record of all industries. Women and men worked in near darkness in tunnels with poor ventilation. They choked from dust raised by chiseling the coal loose and transporting it. There were rats and no provisions for getting rid of human waste. They had to work or navigate in passages that were sometimes less than three feet high and were often partially filled with water.

In these difficult conditions women performed a variety of tasks. Some were hurriers, responsible for loading small wagons with coal and pushing them to the place where they would be taken to the surface. Eleven-year-old Eliza Coats, who hurried with her brother, said that the job made her arms and back sore. Some women worked as drawers or putters. They crawled on their hands and knees while pulling trucks of coal.

Children strain beneath heavy loads of clay in a brickyard in this English illustration.

A coal truck was attached to a woman's body by a chain that ran between her legs and clamped onto a wide leather belt that she wore around her waist. Other women worked as bearers, carrying baskets of coal weighing over a hundred pounds through passages and up ladders to the earth's surface. Young girls, and sometimes boys, between five and eight years old worked as trappers, opening and shutting the doors that controlled ventilation in the tunnels. Trappers were the first into the mines in the morning and the last out at night and often worked in pitch darkness. Joan Perkin cites the experience of one trapper: "Sarah

Gooder, aged eight, a 'trapper' in a Yorkshire mine (she opened the air-door to allow waggons to pass through) said, 'It does not tire me, but I have a trap without a light, and I'm scared. Sometimes I sing when I have a light, but not in the dark; I dare not sing then. I don't like being in the pit.'"[68]

Women and children worked in the mines between twelve and sixteen hours a day. Women were paid about half of what men were paid for the same jobs. Such inequity was perfectly legal. In 1842 Parliament passed an act outlawing underground work by women and girls. In reality, however, many women continued to work underground because there were not enough other jobs for women in their areas. Women were allowed to continue working aboveground sorting coal by the size of the lumps.

Objections to Female Miners

There were those who objected to women working as miners. Some men were disturbed that women sometimes wore trousers and did strenuous labor near men. One mine inspector was particularly concerned because miners and their children were dirty and so were their houses. One report warned that mine work would impair women's ability to bear children and hamper their maternal and domestic instincts. Mine work, the report went on, might "destroy that purity and delicacy of character which ought ever to invest her

with a hallowed atmosphere."[69] Others feared for the morals of women since the men often wore the absolute minimum of clothes in mines. An 1842 report on employment of children records an interview with seventeen-year-old Patience Kershaw:

> The getters [men who actually dug coal from the seams] that I work for are *naked* except their caps; they pull off all their clothes; I see them at work when I go up; Sometimes they beat me, if I am not quick enough, with their hands; they strike me upon my back; the boys take liberties with me sometimes, they pull me about; I am the only girl in the pit; there are about 20 boys and 15 men; all the men are naked; I would rather work in a mill than in a coal-pit.[70]

Women were often raped by the male miners, but there was nothing to do about it when that happened; authorities gave little or no attention to such incidents.

Victorian women endured difficult physical conditions in agriculture, in manufacturing, and in mining. They had little power, little money, and little opportunity to improve their circumstances. Their best hope resided with a small number of social reformers and union leaders who fought to improve the conditions for women working in industry.

Chapter 5:
Women Philanthropists and Reformers

Victorian women played a vital role in the social and political life of the nineteenth century. Their work covered a wide range of activities, from organized philanthropy to political activism aimed at changing government policies. Their work helped to improve conditions in prisons, housing for the poor, employment, and education for women and to advance woman's rights.

Middle-Class Philanthropy

With the decline of agriculture and the movement of large numbers of people to manufacturing towns and large cities, the numbers of urban poor grew enormously. The plight of the poor fostered an outburst of philanthropic work by middle-class women. Hannah More and her sister Martha, for example, opened schools for village children. Others provided remedies to the sick, ran soup kitchens for the poor, worked in charities where poor women had their babies, and helped in asylums for the deaf, blind, destitute, and insane. Women offered the poor advice on homemaking, nursing, and child care.

As time went on, some middle-class women who had done charitable work came to believe that poverty could only

Victorian philanthropist Hannah More opened schools for poor urban children.

Elizabeth Fry's Effect on Newgate Prison

In *Strong-Minded Women and Other Voices from Nineteenth-Century England,* Janet Horowitz Murray reprints a letter written by an anonymous gentleman describing the changes in Newgate Prison after Elizabeth Fry had brought clothing for the prisoners and order to their lives. More than anything it was Fry's warmth and sympathy that made the changes possible.

I went, and requested permission to see Mrs. Fry, which was shortly obtained, and I was conducted by a turnkey to the entrance of the women's wards. On my approach, no loud or dissonant sounds or angry voices indicated that I was about to enter a place, which, I was credibly assured, had long had for one of its titles, that of "Hell above ground." The courtyard, into which I was admitted, instead of being peopled with beings scarcely human, blaspheming, fighting, tearing each other's hair, or gaming with a filthy pack of cards, for the very clothes they wore, which often did not suffice even for decency, presented a scene where stillness and propriety reigned. I was conducted by a decently-dressed person, the newly appointed yard's-woman, to the door of a ward, where, at the head of a long table, sat a lady belonging to the Society of Friends. She was reading aloud to about sixteen women prisoners, who were engaged in needlework around it. Each wore a clean looking blue apron and bib; with a ticket, having a number on it, suspended from her neck by a red tape. They all rose on my entrance, curtsied respectfully, and then, at a signal given, resumed their seats and employments. Instead of a scowl, leer, or ill-suppressed laugh, I observed upon their countenances an air of self-respect and gravity, a sort of consciousness of their improved character, and the altered position in which they were placed. I afterwards visited the other wards, which were the counterparts of the first.

be addressed by social reforms. They had already learned how to run meetings, raise money, look after accounts, and gain publicity; now many put these skills to work as they formed organizations whose purpose was to tackle social problems. Two such organizations were the Women Guardians' Society, which tried to improve workhouse conditions, and the Women's Protective and Provident League, which sought to provide safeguards for women in industry.

Social Reformers

Among the conditions that social reformers tried to address was the treatment of women in English jails. For example,

This woodcut depicts Elizabeth Fry's 1817 visit to London's Newgate Prison. Fry greatly improved conditions for the prison's female inmates.

Elizabeth Fry attacked the problem in Newgate Prison in London, where women prisoners were housed—along with their children. Fry brought in clothes, set a school for the children, and organized activities for the women, which helped reduce the fighting and chaos in the prison. She organized the Ladies' Associations for the Improvement of Female Prisoners and set up a network of committees to work toward reforms in other women's prisons throughout the country.

Other women working for social reforms recognized the need for improvement in slums. There, young boys ran wild and vandalized property. Mary Carpenter pioneered charitable work in these neighborhoods. When she realized that nothing was being done for the slum children, she set up a school for wild street boys. Carpenter and her fellow reformers were largely responsible for passage of the Youthful Offenders Act of 1854, a law that authorized the establishment of reform schools. She also started industrial schools to provide vocational training for poor children. The Industrial Schools Acts of 1857, 1861, and 1866 were largely based on Carpenter's ideas.

Upper-Class Philanthropy

Although upper-class women had been most active in offering personal charity,

Women of Victorian England

after 1880 they joined middle-class women in organized philanthropic work. Besides giving what they could afford in the form of cash, upper-class women used their network of social contacts to sponsor fundraisers such as charity balls and bazaars on their country estates or at their London houses. Finally, aristocratic women lent their names to charitable organizations because posting their names as leader, president, or patron added prestige to causes and made it easier to persuade others to donate.

By midcentury, reformers had made a good start, but some organizations duplicated the services of others, and some needs were left unmet. In July 1857 forty-three social-reform leaders passed a resolution providing for closer coordination among the organizations that were working for social improvement. The women leaders, called the Langham Place Circle, used their skills to form new organizations for the causes that needed attention and to train women to run them.

Employment Reform

The problem of low wages, poor working conditions, and the lack of employment opportunities for working-class women came to the attention of the Langham Place Circle. In 1859 Jessie Boucherett, Barbara Leigh Smith Bodichon, and Bessie Rayner Parkes founded the Society for Promoting the Employ-

ment of Women. They formed an information source of referrals, training, and short-term educational loans for training in skilled lower-middle-class jobs such as bookkeeping, law copying, typewriting, and telegraphy. The society also helped women of higher social ranking who needed to work because some misfortune had resulted in a loss of income. The objective was to provide them with jobs consistent with the lifestyle they were used to "to preserve the habits, the dress, and the countless moral and material associations of the rank to which they were born."[71]

Each of the leaders of the Langham Place Circle set out to recruit other women to work on causes and to inform the public about the need for reforms. They used their writing, public speaking, organizational, and research skills to advance this agenda. For example, in 1866 Jessie Boucherett founded the *Englishwoman's Review*, which focused attention on issues especially relevant to women's employment. This publication went on to become the leading magazine for the feminist movement in England.

Emily Faithful, who was also a member of the Langham Place Circle, used her organizational skills to establish a printing company called Victoria Press, where women were taught typesetting skills, and then Faithful employed them in her company. Victoria Press became the printer for the *English Woman's Journal,* and in 1863 Faithful founded *Victoria Magazine* and in 1877 the *West London Express.* Only women typesetters worked on these three periodicals. Primarily through the work of Faithful, the number of women printers increased in the ten years after 1861 from 419 to 741.

Reformers knew that if their efforts were ever going to change the lives of the working poor, leaders had to emerge from within the ranks of the poor. Margaret Llewelyn Davies, an upper-class woman, used her public speaking talent and organizing ability for this cause. She worked through the Women's Co-operative Guild. She taught the women in this guild effective public speaking techniques and skills for organizing recruitment drives. As the women refined their skills, they campaigned for the improvement of maternal and infant care for the poor, increased minimum wages for employees working in cooperatives, woman suffrage, reform for better housing, and fairer divorce laws. During the twelve years that Davies worked with the Women's Co-operative Guild, it grew to include sixty-seven thousand women in fourteen hundred branches. Some of the volunteers from the guild also helped working women organize the trade union movement.

While Davies was working with the Women's Co-operative Guild, she used her investigative skills in her work as a lobbyist. She was a careful investigator, who went into the worst slums and gathered information about wages, housing conditions, numbers of children, and women's feelings about their lives. She listened to what these women said. She urged women to write their stories if they could write; if they could not, she had others record them. Because the women trusted Davies, they spoke honestly about their lives. "There was a warmth and affection about her [Davies] which never suggested condescension to those less privileged, but rather encouragement and hope."[72] Davies used the stories she gathered to lobby members of Parliament to pass laws that helped poor mothers.

Women's Trade Unions

Other women reformers helped working-class women form organizations such as trade unions to work on their own behalf. Emma Patterson was one of the reformers who devoted her energy to the cause of working women. She founded the Women's Protective and Provident League in 1874, an organization that helped working women form unions. Patterson first helped the bookbinders establish a union and then helped women upholsterers, shirt makers, tailors, and dressmakers establish unions. Patterson also wanted to spread the word that women

This drawing depicts women learning to be typists at the Society for Promoting the Employment of Women, an agency that provided job training for needy women.

needed their own unions. To achieve this objective she founded the monthly *Women's Union Journal* and established the Women's Printing Society to print it. Because of her success in organizing women, Patterson gained respect from male union organizers, who allowed her to be the first woman delegate to the formerly all-male Trade Union Conference in 1875.

Another social reformer, Annie Wood Besant, helped the women's trade union movement by using her writing ability.

In 1888 she published an article entitled "The 'White Slavery' of London Match Workers." In an ironic tone, she detailed how the company owned by Bryant and May was able to pay shareholders high dividends because it forced young girls to work long hours, provided them with little food, and paid them low wages. At the end she called for a boycott of the company. The readers responded, and several hundred match workers gained enough confidence from that response to

Women Philanthropists and Reformers

Women's Obvious Need for Money

In "Letters to Women on Money Earning," published in *Alexandra Magazine* in December 1864, reformer Bessie Rayner Parkes spells out in a pseudorighteous tone why women need to earn money. Her letter is reprinted in Phillipa Levine's book *Victorian Feminism, 1850–1900*.

Let us therefore, first ask ourselves what earning of money really means, when the idea is peeled to its simplest meaning. It implies the helping to produce something useful or otherwise desirable, in exchange for which people will willingly give money. And if women can render useful service to society, either in direct way of production, or by contributing to art, or literature, or education, they certainly ought to do so. There is nothing in the idea itself either degrading, or which is more to the present purpose, *unfeminine*.

strike. The community gathered four hundred pounds to create a fund so that strikers could hold out long enough to gain substantial pay increases. Efforts like those of Patterson and Besant were just what feminist Emilia F.S. Dilke encouraged her fellow upper- and middle-class women to provide when she wrote in the *Fortnightly Review* in 1889:

What we want is not so much money as personal help. Personal influence in carrying on this kind of work means everything. If only the richer, idler, abler women amongst us would come out and help! Teach these poor souls to trust you; show cause why they should, by honestly attempting to understand the complicated difficulties of their labouring lives, and you will find that this gospel of self-defence, which is also one of self-sacrifice, goes to the heart of all those who are truly familiar with the cruel hardships of the working woman's life.[73]

Education Reform

Even as some Victorian women sought to obtain decent wages and working conditions for those in the working class, others sought to improve their own station by increasing their access to educational opportunities. Many Victorian men and even some women opposed such reforms because they genuinely believed that women had inferior minds and should be confined to the domestic world of wife, mother, and homemaker. In an 1884 article in *Chambers's Journal,* an anonymous male writer warned of the dangers of educating women:

Every one of them . . . ought to be trained in conformity with the supreme law of her being, to prove a real helpmate to the man that takes her to wife. . . .

The woman not over- but mis-educated is becoming an alarmingly fruitful cause of the downward tendencies of much of our middle-class society. . . . She cannot sew to any purpose. If she deign to use a needle at all, it is to embroider a smoking-cap for a lover or a pair of slippers for papa. To sew on a button, or cut out and unite the plainest piece of male or female clothing, is not always within her powers. . . .

No philosophy, no tinkering of the constitution, no success in the misnamed higher walks of life and knowledge, will atone for the failure of the mother . . . and if she fail as a mother, she fails as a woman and as a human being. She becomes a mere rag, a tatter of nature's cast-off clothing, spiritless, aimless, a failure in this great world of work. [74]

Attitudes such as these were widespread and helped to explain why women were excluded from major institutions of higher learning. Moreover, there were fears that education would blur the differences between men and women and that educated women would refuse to be mothers and homemakers. Despite such opinions, education for girls and women improved dramatically during the second half of the century.

The revolution in female education began in the 1840s with the founding of two colleges for women. The Governesses' Benevolent Institution founded Queen's College to improve the preparation of young women who would serve

In the mid–nineteenth century, universities began to admit female students like this one.

as governesses. The wealthy widow Elizabeth Raid founded Bedford College to offer girls the same curriculum as boys and to meet the same rigorous standards as male students. Bedford soon became affiliated with the University of London because Bedford graduates proved to be well prepared for university courses. In the years that followed, the University of London became a leader in offering educational opportunities to women. Gradually other universities admitted women, but these students still struggled to receive degrees. Women studied the same curriculum and took the same exams as men, but they were only granted certificates of having completed requirements for the degree because male administrators opposed the concept of equality between men and women.

Eventually, Victorian women made progress against such attitudes. By the end of Victoria's reign, England had twelve universities and colleges that admitted women and granted them formal degrees. It was a new world that bright women hardly dared to believe was real, as Lilian Faithful said about her education at Oxford: "To women, more than to men, the delight of having three years in which to be selfishly absorbed in intellectual pursuits was unspeakable."[75]

The Struggle for Woman's Rights

Just as Victorian women fought for opportunity to obtain an advanced education, they fought to obtain legal rights for themselves. At the beginning of the Victorian

Medical Students Face Hostility

Women trying to attend classes in medical school faced hostility from male students and professors. In a letter to reformer Emily Davis, a Miss Colborne describes what happened when she tried to attend a lecture in physiology. Her letter is reprinted in Philippa Levine's *Victorian Feminism, 1850–1900*.

As the lecturer was explaining something when I entered, he did not discover me until the looks and coughs of the students had attracted his attention to my corner—he broke off in his lecture, and said he should like to decide whether the lecture should be continued or not, there was a show of hands against the continuance, the lecturer then bowed, pronounced the lecture discontinued, and the students left the room. I intend to try the Chemistry lecture tomorrow morning.

era, women in England basically had no rights. As late as 1878, reformist Frances Power Cobbe ruled against women's legal standing: "The notion that a man's wife is his PROPERTY, in the sense in which a horse is his property . . . is the fatal root of incalculable evil and misery." [76]

In 1854 Barbara Leigh Smith Bodichon published a pamphlet outlining the low status of women in the eyes of the law. She explained the legal position of women in clear, simple language. When a woman married, her husband owned her body. He owned all of her property, including her jewels, her clothes, and her inheritance from her parents, and he had the right to sell any of her property, even if he and the wife were not living together. Any money a woman earned from working belonged to her husband. A husband was not obligated to support his wife. A woman could make a will if her husband permitted her to do so, but he could withdraw that permission whenever he wished, making the will invalid. In the event of separation, women had no rights to custody of children, except for a few months when they were infants, and husbands could take away children already living with mothers. Because women were considered property, they could not sign contracts, nor were they responsible for excessive spending or theft. Finally, men had the right to force women to obey their demands, even by physical means. Bodichon's list set off the

Social reformer Frances Power Cobbe tirelessly promoted woman's rights.

first move among feminists to organize. Shortly after, Bodichon and Bessie Rayner Parkes gathered twenty-six thousand signatures on a petition asking Parliament to grant wives the right to financial independence.

Women were legally disadvantaged even in cases of severe domestic abuse. Writer Caroline Norton, for example, suffered abuse from her husband, George. He first kicked her because she told him one of his ideas was silly, and similar physical abuse recurred over a nine-year period.

She periodically stayed at her mother's house, but she returned home each time because her three sons were there. When they separated permanently, George refused to tell Norton where the children were living. Norton began a campaign to change child custody laws by writing a pamphlet in 1837 that included details of several cases of abuse. After reading Norton's document, a progressive member of Parliament introduced a bill to give women the right to see their children, but it was thrown out in the House of Lords, which was the upper house of Parliament. Norton wrote another pamphlet, *A Plain Letter to the Lord Chancellor on the Infant Custody Bill,* which she signed with a man's name, and sent it to every member of the House of Lords. This time, in 1839, a limited bill passed, giving courts power to grant a mother access to her infant children and custody of those under seven years of age. Reformer Harriet Martineau said this act was the first blow struck at the oppression of Victorian wives.

Throughout the 1870s and 1880s, women reformers campaigned for woman's rights. In 1878 reformer Frances Power Cobbe wrote an article, "Wife Torture in England," in which she pointed out that in England wife beating was taken as a joke, and wives were portrayed as nags and scolds while judges treated husbands' abuse as petty. She said, "The proceeding [of wife abuse] seems to be surrounded by a certain halo of jocosity [humor] which

inclines people to smile whenever they hear of a case of it."[77] Her campaign led to passage of the Matrimonial Causes Act, which allowed an abused wife to separate from her husband and if he was convicted of aggravated assault, to receive maintenance payments. Another reformer, Ursula Bright, who was married to a progressive member of Parliament, worked from 1874 until 1882 for passage of the Married Women's Property Act. The passage of this act in 1882 finally gave women the right to own property.

Women who campaigned for the rights of women were accused of being against marriage. This, however, was not the case. As historian Philippa Levine says, "They did not seek, as critics constantly claimed, to undermine the practice or prevalence of marriage but to realign the rights of partners within that institution."[78]

The Contagious Diseases Acts

Victorian reformers continually worked to eliminate inequities in public policy. A major goal for them was the repeal of the Contagious Diseases Acts of 1864, 1866, and 1869. These acts were the work of military officers concerned about the spread of venereal disease among soldiers and sailors. The acts required periodic genital examinations by male doctors of any woman suspected of being a prostitute who lived near a large military installation. Women who were found to have a sexually transmitted disease were placed in locked hospital wards. The lesions caused by syphilis and gonorrhea were treated with mercury ointment, despite the fact that this treatment caused painful burning and sometimes caused kidney damage. Women who refused inspection were imprisoned and were sometimes forced to do hard labor. Only women were required to be examined; a military doctor said the examination of soldiers "would tend to destroy the men's self-respect."[79] Reformer Josephine Butler took up the cause of the prostitutes. She worked tirelessly for repeal of the Contagious Diseases Acts by writing articles and speaking in public forums. In 1870 she wrote a petition to Parliament protesting the acts, which 251 prominent women signed. Finally, in response to Butler's efforts, Parliament abolished the acts in 1880.

The Fight for Woman Suffrage

Among the causes championed by reformers, the one that they all agreed on was woman suffrage. Reformers lobbied, spoke publicly, and wrote articles, eventually obtaining the right to vote in local elections and to hold minor local offices. Still, the vote was granted only to married women and to those who owned property, and reformers fought against these restrictions.

Just how hard they should push for voting rights was a point of disagreement among feminists. It was Emmeline Pankhurst, who chose to take a militant, single-minded approach to the suffrage question. Pankhurst had worked with poor women who had been deserted by their husbands. She obtained a position on the Board of Poor Law Guardians, an agency governing workhouses, hospitals, welfare, and schools for the poor. As a member of the board, she realized that the laws as they were written were ineffective, and that politicians were unlikely to make necessary changes until women could make themselves heard by voting.

Pankhurst started a militant movement, the Women's Social and Political Union, whose members were called the suffragettes. The movement focused entirely on a campaign for the right to vote. Women who joined the movement had to promise to work on this one issue alone. They made banners with their slogan, Vote for Women, and took them to the streets and to Parliament. In her own story, Pankhurst describes taking the cause to the public:

> We had a lot of suffrage literature printed, and day by day our members went forth and held street meetings. Selecting a favourable spot, with a chair for a rostrum, one of us would ring a bell until people began to stop to see what was going to happen. What happened, of course, was a lively suffrage speech, and the distribution

In this 1904 photo, women representing various professions rally for woman suffrage as policemen watch.

Many people dismissed Pankhurst as a fanatic, but thousands of women shared her opinion that contemporary conventional politics were unable to address women's interests. As hard as women worked for the right to vote, it took until 1918 for women over age thirty to get the vote and until 1928 for the voting age for women to be lowered to twenty-one.

Most Victorian reformers were women of some wealth and privilege who could have conformed to the ideal role of wife, mother, and homemaker. Instead, they chose lives of writing, organizing, speaking, and campaigning for others whose lives were hard and dismal. For their choices, they often endured the criticism of fellow Victorians, both men and some women. By the end of the century, women had made progress toward better conditions for themselves. Some were unwilling to quit until they had fully eliminated inequity from Victorian society. In speaking on justice for women, reformer Millicent Garrett Fawcett said, "We have gone so far and with such good results there could hardly be a better reason for going farther."[81]

of literature. Soon after our campaign had started, the sound of the bell was a signal for a crowd to spring up as if by magic. All over the neighbourhood you heard the cry: "Here come the Suffragettes! Come on!" We covered London in this way; we never lacked an audience.[80]

In the course of the campaign, women were arrested and fined. When some who had been thrown in jail staged a hunger strike, they were force-fed.

Chapter 6:
Women Entertainers

As the British economy grew during the Victorian era, more people had money to spend on entertainment, creating an increasing demand for singers and actors. In 1841, for example, the census showed 387 actresses; in 1911, it showed 9,171. In many ways entertainers had greater freedom than the ideal Victorian homemaker or the working woman and more opportunities for intellectual and creative expression.

Women entertainers played an important part in Victorian England's cultural life at all levels of society. Upper-class men and women gathered in London during May, June, and July to attend operas and plays—in which women sang and acted in key roles. Those in the middle-class rarely attended these performances since they generally had neither the income nor the social connections to be welcomed to events attended by the upper class. Instead, they attended performances designed to appeal to middle-class tastes. The working class, meanwhile, frequented music halls where women performed in dance routines and sang popular songs.

Opera and Operetta Singers

In a way, Britain's entertainers reflected society as a whole. Many of the most talented opera singers performed at the Royal Opera House at Covent Garden in central London. There, they had the opportunity to enjoy the best of working conditions. They performed on beautiful sets, wore fine costumes, and were accompanied by a talented orchestra. They enjoyed the undivided attention of audiences while they were on stage. One famous opera singer, Nellie Melba, regularly sang in operas at Covent Garden. A soprano, she was adept at singing opera's most demanding roles. Her talent brought her fame worldwide. When she was not entertaining the London upper class during the social season, she sang at Italy's most famous opera house, La Scala, and at the Metropolitan Opera in New York.

Other talented singers performed in palaces before royalty or in London's famous cathedrals. Rather than opera, these singers performed oratorios, lengthy vocal works that demanded many of the same qualities of singers, such as vocal range and ability to project one's voice, as opera did. Clara Novello was a soprano who was well known as a distinguished oratorio singer. From the 1830s to the 1850s, she sang works by composers Ludwig van Beethoven, Felix Mendelssohn, and George Handel.

Both opera and oratorio soloists had educational opportunities not available to

Victorian opera singer Nellie Melba enjoyed worldwide acclaim.

most Victorian women. They had studied the works of the world's most famous composers and had the benefit of extensive voice training. Even those who were not soloists enjoyed opportunities to live well, if they were talented enough. Both operas and oratorios required large choruses that required women to sing alto and soprano parts. Although members of the chorus did not enjoy the fame of the soloists, compared with the working conditions endured by most Victorian women, these singers were fortunate.

Other women entertainers performed before middle-class audiences, combining singing and acting by performing in operettas, which became a popular form of entertainment in the late 1860s. Like opera singers, performers in operettas worked in theaters with sets, costumes, and orchestras. Among the more popular operettas were those written and produced by Arthur Sullivan and William Gilbert. The operettas the pair produced were satires; for example, *Trial by Jury* satirized the British legal system, *H.M.S. Pinafore* satirized the navy, and *Princess Ida* satirized the feminist movement. Gilbert and Sullivan employed a large number of young female singers and trained them. Gilbert, especially, watched over these young women to protect their reputations. Gilbert came to be called "the Dramatic Daddy," and the Savoy Theater, where his works were performed, "the Savoy Boarding School."

Music Hall Entertainers

While the upper and middle classes found their musical entertainment in the formal settings of operas, oratorios, and operettas, the working class attended the more raucous, partylike music halls. There, women entertained audiences with singing and dancing acts and often interacted with those audience members seated near the stage. Music hall entertainers had little in the way of formal music or voice training, but some singers were able to captivate an audience and were extremely popular.

Working conditions in music halls changed drastically over the years. In the 1830s and 1840s women performed in a room adjacent to a pub and the audience consisted of drinking men. Men would stand close to the stage and try to grope the women as they performed. By the 1880s music halls had been designed and built that were much like the best London theaters. Drinking was no longer allowed, and members of the audience sat in rows. The audiences changed as well. Instead of drunken men, audiences tended to consist of men and women who came to enjoy performance of popular songs of the day.

In almost all of their performances, these women conveyed underlying, often sexual messages with their body movements or in the lines they sang. An ability to connect with the audience emotionally was of great importance. One of the most unforgettable music hall performers was Marie Lloyd, who started singing in 1885 in the West End music halls. She sang about love, poverty, and the hard life in such songs as "The Boy in the Gallery" and "The Piccadilly Trot." Historian Wilson J. Hoffman notes this about her: "Though not beautiful or of outstanding voice, she had charisma, flair, spirit, and the rare ability to establish rapport with audiences. She titillated audiences not with words but with well-timed suggestive motions (her wink was her trademark)."[82]

Women Theater Managers

Some women parlayed their stage success into success in business. Talented performers who also managed theaters had opportunities that only the wealthiest women enjoyed otherwise. They could express their creative and intellectual abilities without the criticism that they were violating the standards that Victorian society set for women. Madame Vestris, born Lucy Elizabeth Bartolozzi, was one such woman who had a combined career as a performer and a theater manager. Vestris was an operatic contralto who also sang comic ballads. She attained her greatest popularity performing in burlesques, works in which the singers perform songs loaded with puns and jokes.

Vestris went on to take management of the small Olympic Theatre on Wych

Madame Vestris enjoyed a successful career as a performer and theater manager.

Street. She had two strategies for making it a success. First, she paid special attention to the sets. Instead of using backdrops painted to look as if the room had walls and furniture, she used real carpets, real hardware, such as doorknobs that turned, and real tables. Audiences liked this kind of realism. Second, she geared performance schedules to the needs of the middle-class audience she wanted to attract, making certain that her patrons could attend during their leisure time.

Vestris was not the only woman who found success both as a performer and as a theater manager. Marie Wilson was a successful actress, and when she tired of acting she borrowed a thousand pounds (highly unusual for a woman in Victorian England) to buy a rundown theater in a poor location. Aware of the audience she hoped to attract, she decorated the theater to suit middle-class tastes turning it into what one social historian describes as a "pink- and blue-draped, upholstered, and carpeted band-box." [83] Wilson, along with her husband, Squire Bancroft, made three major changes that changed theater going for the British middle class. First, they produced one play per night, instead of two or three shorter shows. This allowed them to concentrate on producing a well-rehearsed, high-quality play. Second, they streamlined the process of attending a play: They set performance time for the convenience of middle-class patrons, and organized orderly lines for the purchase of tickets. They also increased ticket prices to attract a higher-class audience and instituted a requirement that patrons wear formal clothing to performances. To further appeal to the tastes of the educated middle class, they required performers to abandon the overly dramatic, exaggerated, and rather silly acting style that had previously been used. Wilson and Bancroft promoted a more natural, understated acting style.

Experimenting with New Plays

Some of the less traditional Victorian actresses aligned themselves with the feminist movement and performed in plays that helped to advance woman's rights. These actresses belonged to a loose association of women, called the New Women, who favored independence and sexual freedom for women. In their private lives, these actresses joined other New Women, defying the Victorian ideal of a woman as wife and homemaker by smoking, drinking, and wearing trousers in public. In their professional lives, they acted in plays by the English playwright George Bernard Shaw and the Norwegian playwright Henrik Ibsen, both of whom wrote plays that explored issues of concern to the New Women. Because their themes were controversial and still unknown to all but a small population of intellectuals, these plays were performed only in small theaters as matinees. Though these actresses did not enjoy the wide popularity that other actresses enjoyed, they did have opportunities to explore new ideas and to pioneer acting styles suited to the new plays.

Victorian Actresses of Many Talents

In "Image and Reality: The Actress and Society," Christopher Kent enumerates the many accomplishments of Victorian women working in the theater. His essay is published in *A Widening Sphere: Changing Roles of Victorian Women,* edited by Martha Vicinus.

The artistic and professional momentum generated in the 1890's was sustained until the eve of World War I as women became more prominent in the theater than ever before (or perhaps since), not only as actresses and audience, but as directors, producers, and playwrights. Janet Achurch, Elizabeth Robins, and Cicely Hamilton were playwrights as well as actresses. Florence Farr, Gertrude Kingston, Lena Ashwell, and Lillah McCarthy became actress-managers, with their own companies and the freedom to produce the experimental and intellectual plays that much better known commercially-minded actor-managers tended to shun. In addition to this greatly increased level of professional participation and artistic responsibility among women in the theater, there was a growing sense of mutuality, reflected in organizations like the Theatrical Ladies Guild, founded in 1891 to assist needy actress-mothers with children's clothes, and struggling actresses with wardrobe.

Entertainers of Light Comedy

Women acting in what at the time was considered experimental theater were in the minority. By the 1890s the majority of actresses worked in theaters where plays catering to popular tastes were staged. These theaters produced light comedies and musicals which, by this time, had emerged as a still lighter alternative to the operetta. These plays had titles like *The Shop Girl* and *The Runaway Girl*. Women acting in these plays were less interested in intellectual and acting challenges and more interested in the public attention they

Most Victorian actresses worked in comedy theaters like the one advertised in this poster.

received for their roles. The women who starred in these plays were beautiful and played daring and exciting parts on stage. The popular newspapers published titillating stories about their private lives, and hawkers peddled postcards bearing pictures of them. Although their performances appealed to the middle class, these actresses were accepted by the upper class. During the thirty years from 1884 to 1914, nineteen actresses married men of the nobility, fourteen of them to members of the House of Lords. Other actresses were friends of noblemen. Cora Brown Potter, for example, was a friend of the Prince of Wales. Another actress, Lily Lantry, was the mistress of the Prince of Wales for a time.

Attitudes Toward Entertainers

Victorian society had a mix of attitudes toward actresses. They were welcomed in most social circles, and theatergoing was a socially acceptable pasttime. Queen Victoria and her husband regularly attended the theater and invited actresses to royal social events. Yet society still saw actresses as somehow less than moral. Social historian Tracy C. Davis notes:

> Irrespective of changes in the socio-economic, educational, or moral background of recruits and despite the theater's increasingly sympathetic reception, popular culture continued to ascribe immorality and sexual indis-

The overtly sexual performances of showgirls like London's Gaiety Girls often clashed with Victorian mores.

violated the dress codes of the street and drawing room, flaunting the ankles, calves, knees, thighs, crotch, and upper torso. Cross-dressing as males was sometimes the pretense, highlighting rather than disguising sexual difference." [85]

The overt sexual content of theatrical performances did not always sit well with Victorian attitudes. Writing in 1839, a Dr. Michael Ryan complained:

> Who has not seen actresses appear in . . . dresses as white as marble, and fitting so tightly that the shape of their bodies could not be more apparent, had they come forward on the stage in a state of nature [naked]? Again, the opera dancers appear nightly before crowded moral audiences, in dresses made for the express purpose of exposing their . . . figure, while the style of dancing is such as to excite the most wanton thoughts and lascivious desires. [86]

cretion to actresses; the stigma existed on the level of common knowledge. [84]

Victorian women entertainers had to struggle against other middle-class attitudes as well. Since Victorians prided themselves on having a serious and rational work ethic, they had trouble imagining that acting could be a serious vocation for either men or women. Moreover, women performers in costumes violated the prevailing standard for appropriate dress. Davis explains: "Theatrical costume flagrantly

Many men who were enamored by the seductive devices of actresses tried to meet them backstage or follow them after they left the theater. Others fantasized about them and purchased weekly newspapers that featured pictures of actresses in erotic poses. For example, three weeklies featured depictions from actual performances of women kicking high in a chorus line or reclining seductively.

Actresses Appear in Weeklies

Actresses appeared in the pictures and stories of sensational newspapers such as *Days' Doings,* which emphasized murder mysteries and daring and unusual feats. A story about a dancer doing a snake dance appeared in the "Dramatic Doings" column. The excerpt is reprinted in *Victorian Scandals,* edited by Kristine Ottesen Garrigan.

To a slimy, creeping tune she glides up to an urn of flowers, and drags there- from a hideous, cussed snake. She shakes the torpid wretch until he slowly unfolds himself, runs his forky tongue out, and wags his scaly tail in long-meter fashion. Then she dances and winds the clammy worm about her neck, and if there's a man in the audience wants to make her acquaintance after [this] exhibition it's some man that owns an anaconda and wants to have it educated.

For their part, actresses themselves took advantage of opportunities to enhance their profession. Marie Wilson worked tirelessly to make the theater a suitable place for families, and in 1884 actress Madge Robertson Kendal was asked to speak at the National Association for the Promotion of Social Science. She took the opportunity to promote acting as an honorable profession. When she was criticized in the press, the acting community and many of her supporters defended the honor of actresses. By the 1890s Victorians had come to recognize that actresses could be both glamorous and respectable.

Furthermore, older actresses found new opportunities that brought them added respect—and income as well. Some gave lessons in public speaking. Others gave public readings of dramatic works. Middle-class Victorians who would not enter a theater out of religious or moral concerns flocked to concert halls to hear actresses Helena Faucit or Fanny Kelly give dramatic readings from poetry, novels, or Shakespeare's works.

Prostitution in London

Victorians were divided in their view of actresses; they were far less so in their attitudes toward another class of women: prostitutes. Still, there were plenty of woman practicing this profession. Exactly how many is unclear. Reformers and journalists of the day estimated that at midcentury London had between sixty and eighty thousand prostitutes, but police figures showed a much smaller number of eight thousand, who likely composed the core of full-time prostitutes. More often, women who worked in low-paid jobs as servants, needleworkers, and laundry workers occasionally engaged in prostitution in order to earn extra cash. Victorians themselves chose to believe that most prostitutes eventually gave up their profession and married. Social historian William Acton said in 1870:

> Most women who have resorted to prostitution for a livelihood return sooner or later to a more or less regular course of life. . . . Incumbrances rarely attend the prostitute who flies from the horror of her position. We must recollect that she has a healthy frame, an excellent constitution, and is in the vigour of life. . . . Is it surprising, then, that she should . . . make a dash at respectability by marriage?[87]

The claim that prostitutes mostly longed for marriage aside, some Victorian women found prostitution to be more attractive than work as servants; as prostitutes, they worked fewer hours, received higher pay, wore more fashionable clothes, and enjoyed drinking and dancing in pubs. The most popular West End prostitutes made more in one night than a working man could earn in a month, the majority of them averaging between twenty and thirty pounds (about eight to twelve hundred dollars) a week.

Courtesans

Vast differences, however, existed in the hierarchy of prostitutes. At the top of the hierarchy were the courtesans, whose clients were men of rank or wealth. Harriette Wilson, known as the "Queen of Tarts," was the most famous and the most popular of all courtesans. Her house was a gathering place for noblemen. Joan Perkin describes her allure:

> Harriette was not the golden-hearted whore of sentimental literature. She was as hard as nails and matey, frank and familiar with her clients, rather than romantic. "Harry" [as she was called] was not staggeringly beautiful, but she had an alluring figure, fine colouring, and abounding vitality. Sir Walter Scott said she was "a

Harriette Wilson, known as the "Queen of Tarts," was the most famous Victorian courtesan.

smart, saucy girl, with good eyes and dark hair, and the manners of a wild schoolboy." [88]

The ambition of many intelligent women who worked as prostitutes was to be a mistress for one well-off man, but this arrangement seldom offered a woman security. Since the law did not even require men to support cast-off wives, mistresses had even fewer grounds for support. Many wealthy men, however, voluntarily supported their mistresses after separation. The actress Dorothy Jordan, for example, was the mistress of the Duke of Clarence for twenty years and had ten children by him. He cast her off and married a princess when he became King William IV, but he remained devoted to the ten children he had with Jordan.

A Prima Donna Star of the Dance Hall

In *Strong-Minded Women and Other Lost Voices from the Nineteenth Century,* Janet Horowitz Murray reprints an excerpt from historian William Acton's book *Prostitutes.* In this excerpt he describes an unnamed prima donna in her star role at the casino, or dancing room.

One woman merits a passing notice here, who has achieved a sudden notoriety, and given to the casino . . . a pre-eminence over its rival. There she holds a mimic court, attired unlike the rest of the frequenters, who come in their bonnets in full ball dress. She is surrounded by a crowd of admirers, idlers, and would-be imitators, and gives the tone to the establishment that she patronizes. It is said that the diamonds worn by this woman are worth 5,000 [pounds]. She is supplied daily from a florist in Covent Garden with a bouquet of the choicest flowers, amid which are interspersed specimens of the most beautifully coloured beetles, the cost being about 30s. [150 pence], and her habit on entering the rooms is to present this really splendid trifle to the female attendant at the wine bar, as a mark of her condescension and favour. On permission to visit her being requested, she would probably, like another celebrated *"fille de joie"* [prostitute], take out her pocketbook and, after a careless glance at it, reply that she was full of engagements, but that if the petitioner would call at her house at a given hour that day week, she would, perhaps, spare him some twenty minutes of her society, for which favour she might expect the modest sum of 25 [pounds].

Women of Victorian England

Prima Donnas and Common Prostitutes

Next down the social hierarchy of prostitutes were the prima donnas. These are women who worked the dance halls, such as the Argyll Room and the Holborn. All of the women were attractive, well dressed in ball gowns, and tastefully made up. A man would introduce himself by buying drinks for a prostitute of his choice; he would then dance with her, arrange to meet at her house, and negotiate a price. A few women had men who regularly met them at the dance hall, but they took other clients when their regular man did not arrive. Dance-hall prima donnas were usually daughters of tradesmen and artisans, or they were workers in shops. Their earnings, between forty and sixty shillings (about $80 and $120) per week, were far higher than their shop pay.

Common prostitutes made up the lowest level in the hierarchy, although they had a hierarchy of their own. Some rented rooms in lodging houses, and their status depended on the part of London where they worked. Other prostitutes worked in towns such as Portsmouth, where large numbers of soldiers and sailors were stationed. These prostitutes worked from the pubs and were supplied a room upstairs in return for encouraging soldiers and sailors to buy large numbers of drinks. The dollymops, inexperienced servant girls or poor girls living at home, tried to earn a little extra money by soliciting clients in parks. One poor fifteen-year-old girl, who regularly had little to eat but gruel, worked as a prostitute so that she could buy sausage rolls, meat pies, and pastry.

Finally, at the bottom of the hierarchy were the thieves' women, who lived on the streets and looked for men to take them in for the night. Historian Henry Mayhew described "three such women standing together, 'innocent of crinoline,' and wearing 'old bonnets and shawls.' They were still prostitutes although their hair was going grey." [89]

Prostitutes were a major concern for the respectable middle class and for reformers. Social reformers pitied prostitutes and tried to help them because they believed they had been ruined by men. Religious reformers saw prostitutes as fallen, sinful women who needed to be saved by religion. Reformer Annie Besant said that if employers paid women living wages, the streets would be emptied of prostitutes.

The work of most women whose roles were to entertain, from the most professional opera and theater performers to the kept women and street prostitutes, soon passed into obscurity. Only a few of these individuals have caught the eye of historians, who have recorded their stories. One class of entertainers would not suffer this fate. The poetry and prose of Victorian women would captivate readers in their own time. And a few writers of the Victorian era would achieve lasting fame.

Chapter 7:
Women Writers

Victorian women wrote volumes of literature, and Victorian women read voraciously. Many Victorian women wrote what was popular with the domestic audience of their time and were quickly forgotten. However, a few women novelists and a couple of women poets achieved prominence during their lifetimes and went on to enjoy lasting fame.

All writers, whether major or minor, faced common conditions and problems stemming from the values of the Victorian era. As middle-class women, few paid career opportunities were available to them; writing was one career that was acceptable to their class. They could work at home, and writing, especially poetry, was considered suited to a woman's temperament.

Forgotten Poets

Most of the women poets were like other women who worked—they wanted a job with comfortable working conditions, and they wanted to earn money. To achieve these goals, they wrote poems about what the public wanted to read and sold them to magazines and weekly newspapers. Since the time they were writing, most of these poets have been forgotten, some because critics of the day ignored them, and some because their poetry lacked the quality to be taken seriously by succeeding generations of readers.

The poets who became popular with mass audiences portrayed traditional middle-class values, such as the duties of wives and mothers. Felicia Hemans is an example of a poet who reinforced the ideal role of women. According to *Blackwood's Edinburgh Magazine* of December 1848, "Her piety, her resignation, her love of nature and of home . . . all speak of the cultivated woman bred under English skies, and in English homes."[90] One of her most popular poems reinforces the Victorian ideal for women by describing adolescent girls taking on their adult roles with a mix of joy and woe.

Some of the poets who have largely been forgotten penned rhymes with simple sentiments in order to please a wide audience. Short poems about the beauty of nature, children playing, or acts of human kindness were often printed with sketches that reinforced the subject of the poem. Women who wrote these poems fulfilled an important function. Because their poems were short, they provided something that a woman could read during a short respite from work. Moreover, because the sentiments were pleasing, the poems gave readers whose own lives were difficult something about which they could momentarily feel good.

While most Victorian women who wrote poetry came from the middle class, a few poets came from the working class. One was Janet Hamilton, the daughter of a Scottish shoemaker. Because she never learned to write, she dictated her poems to her husband and son, who recorded them for her. Speaking in a Scottish dialect, she made poems about women's work and the evils of drink. She was well known locally but never gained a national reputation. Another working-class poet was Ellen Johnston, a Scottish woman known as "the Factory Girl" because she had worked in a factory from age eight. She wrote about her hard life and sold her poems and her autobiography to help support herself and her illegitimate daughter.

Defying Expectations

A few Victorian women poets defied society's expectations. For example, Vic-torian poets Elizabeth Barrett Browning and Christina Rossetti both achieved lasting fame writing, not for the mass market, but for other poets and scholars. In their works they confronted issues of particular importance to Victorian women, such as education and marriage and the feminist response to these issues.

Both Browning and Rossetti were sensitive to the expectation that women

A poet is hard at work in this mid-nineteenth-century painting.

become wives and homemakers. As educated women, both poets sympathized with the goals of feminism, but they identified with feminists in different ways. Browning saw herself as an advocate for women's freedom and for poor and working women. She addressed these issues openly in her poetry, writing, for example, about poverty and prostitution. Rossetti, on the other hand, shunned reformers and feminists and adhered to the traditional image of a woman who is subordinate to a man. She focused on topics of private, not public, concern. Critics have identified her as a poet of the inner self, a poet of feeling, a poet who hid herself, and a poet of the dark side of human nature.

Browning criticized the inequality between men and women and the limited roles imposed on Victorian women. For example, on the surface, her forty-five poems entitled *Sonnets from the Portuguese* appear to be simple expressions of her deep feelings for her husband. Taken together, however, the poems identify a

The poems of Elizabeth Barrett Browning (left) and Christina Rosetti deal largely with Victorian attitudes toward women.

The Hard Work of Writing

In Elizabeth Barrett Browning's narrative poem *Aurora Leigh,* the main character, Leigh, is a writer. In this excerpt from book 3, Browning, in Leigh's words, expresses the hard work that an artist's life requires.

I worked on, on.
Through all the bristling fence of
　nights and days
Which hedges time in from the
　eternities,
I struggled,—never stopped to note
　the stakes

Which hurt me in my course. The
　midnight oil
Would stink sometimes; there came
　some vulgar needs:
I had to live that therefore I might
　work,
And, being but poor, I was constrained,
　for life,
To work with one hand for the
　booksellers
While working with the other for
　myself
And art.

loving, equal, and supportive relationship between her husband and herself, as if to say that this way is better than the middle-class ideal of female dependency that was widely accepted in her time.

In her most ambitious work, the narrative poem titled *Aurora Leigh,* she criticizes Victorian attitudes toward women and the treatment of them. Literary scholar Kathleen Hickok says that in the story, Browning

explored virtually all the women's roles with which the public was familiar in mid-nineteenth-century England. By considering the poem's female characters in terms of their social roles and in light of the accompanying feminist commentary upon women in general which Aurora provides, we discover the full force of the poem: *Aurora Leigh* rejects the conventional wisdom about women at virtually every point.[91]

Browning chose characters from each of the classes of Victorian society and then commented on them and their actions. Lady Waldemar, the villain, is from the upper class; Aurora Leigh, a writer, is from the middle class; and Marian Erle, a prostitute turned seamstress, is from the lower class. Romney Leigh rescues Erle from prostitution and helps her become a seamstress, but Erle and her daughter still live in poverty until Aurora Leigh rescues her from her plight. Romney Leigh wants to marry Aurora, his cousin, but she chooses her writing over marriage. The story involves many events and several other characters, but in the end Aurora marries Romney, but only when he accepts her in a loving, equal relationship. Through this narrative written in poetic form, she expresses her strong view that women should be free and treated with justice and love.

Despite her view of herself as a poet who expressed her inner thoughts and emotions, not as a social critic, several of Christina Rossetti's poems sharply criticize contemporary situations and injustices. Elizabeth K. Helsinger and her fellow critics call Rossetti "a restless and assertive self operating behind the mask of genteel composure and protesting against women's dependence on man." [92] Some of her poems, such as the ones about death and aging, are indeed poems about individual feelings, but others make pointed statements about Victorian society. For example, when the princess in "A Royal Princess" tosses her gold and jewels to a mob of poor people, Rossetti gives prominence to the wide economic gap between the upper and lower classes.

Like all Victorian writers, Rossetti was severely constrained in dealing with topics like sex and male-female relationships. In response, Rossetti and her colleagues resorted to highly symbolic language. For example in "Goblin Market" she creates a scenario in which two young women buy fruit at the market. There, they are confronted by two goblins, who are symbolic of sexually aggressive men and who tempt the girls to buy their "fruit":

> The whisk-tailed merchant bade
>   her taste
> In tones as smooth as honey,
> The cat-faced purr'd
> The rat-paced spoke a word
> Of welcome, and the snail-paced
>   even was heard;
> One parrot-voiced and jolly
> Cried "Pretty Goblin" still for
>   "Pretty Polly";—
> One whistled like a bird. [93]

Rossetti gives humanlike qualities to the fruits, which represent eroticism:

> Plump unpecked cherries . . .
> Bloom-down-cheeked peaches,
> Swart-headed mulberries,
> Wild free-born cranberries. [94]

By using symbolism, Rossetti makes the temptation experienced by the girls and the sexual abuse inflicted by the men both vivid and disgusting. At the same time, by making the poem appear to be about events at a market, she circumvents the Victorian taboo on discussing sex.

Domestic Novels

Just as Victorian women produced both superficial or serious poetry, so too did they write novels of varying degrees of seriousness. The works written to please mass audiences are known as domestic novels. In these works, the novelists affirm the common manners of middle-class society. The heroines of these novels have high morals and live a life of duty and selflessness in a selfish world. Literary critics Helsinger, Robin Lauterbach Sheets, and William Veeder explain, "From the 1820s well into the 1860s, commentators urge the novelists to create noble, self-sacrificing female characters; to affirm the truth of the affections, the sanctity of the home, and the importance of religion; and to provide detailed descriptions of everyday life."[95] Charlotte Yonge typifies the writer of the domestic novel with the one that made her famous, *The Heir of Redclyffe.* In it she portrays religious young girls going to parties and balls and doing needlework. Her characters are vibrant, and Yonge makes virtuous behavior seem interesting.

Women novelists enlarged the vision of the domestic novel when they incorporated themes of social reform. In these stories, they subtly attack the notion that a woman's place is in the home and that dominance and power should be reserved for men. Elizabeth Gaskell was typical of this group. When her son died from scarlet fever, in her grief she became conscious of the suffering of others. To express her new awareness, she began writing. Her first novel, *Mary Barton: A Tale of a Manchester Life,* which portrays the life of a factory girl, was attacked as unfair to employers, but Gaskell kept writing. *Cranfield,* her novel sympathizing with the plight of aging single women, found greater acceptance. In 1853 she published *Ruth,* the story of an unmarried mother who is befriended by the minister Thurston Benson.

Gaskell's sympathetic portrayal of a woman who violates Victorian norms outraged some who felt the main character should have been treated more harshly. Gaskell's experience was by no means

Victorian novelist Elizabeth Gaskell's works promoted social reform.

unique. All domestic novelists had to be cautious that their stories stayed within the limits of acceptable middle-class values. If a story's characters strayed outside the bounds of what was considered proper, the book might be banned, or the reading public might simply refuse to buy a novel that it felt was critical of them and their values. Gaskell expressed her disappointment at the reaction of people in her community:

> I think I must be an improper woman without knowing it, I do so manage to shock people. Now *should* you have burnt the 1st vol. of Ruth as so *very* bad? even if you had been a very anxious father of a family? Yet *two* men have; and a third has forbidden his wife to read it; they sit next to us in Chapel and you can't think how "improper" I feel under their eyes. [96]

Several circulating libraries banned the book.

Artistic Novels

Some Victorian women set their sights on writing novels meant not merely to please a mass audience but also to compare favorably with the best novels written by men. They wanted to tell the truth about their society as they saw it without regard to social conventions. They wanted to develop their own artistic approach to literary elements such as structure, character, and point of view. They found, however, that gaining attention as serious novelists posed some hurdles. Kathryn Gleadle notes some of the problems:

> Yet even the most successful female writers had to pick their way through a complex maze of gendered assumptions. Social convention meant that women frequently felt obliged to insist that they did not write for money. Many female writers chose to adopt male pseudonyms because of the widespread bias as to the intellectual and artistic capabilities of women.... [They] found it difficult to project themselves as professional authors. [97]

Three novelists—Emily Brontë, Charlotte Brontë, and Mary Ann Evans—chose to write novels that fulfilled their goals despite the hurdles. Their works have achieved lasting fame.

Emily Brontë disregarded convention in producing her one novel, *Wuthering Heights,* but the book was badly received by reviewers. They criticized her for using two narrative characters and for portraying the lovers Catherine and Heathcliff, whose passion burns, as literary scholar Muriel Masefield notes, "with an almost unearthly fire which owes nothing to sensuality." [98] The first reviewers were hostile, as critic Joanne Shattock notes, "by what they saw as the ferocity and the improbability of the characters, the coarseness of the language, and the author's apparent

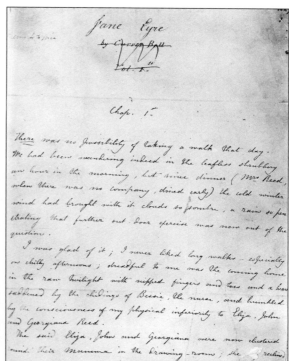

Charlotte Brontë wrote her most famous novel, Jane Eyre, *under the pseudonym Currer Bell, as seen on the manuscript's title page.*

lack of a clear moral viewpoint." [99] Eventually, however, critics came to praise Brontë's imagination, the power of her language, and the complexity of her characters.

Emily Brontë's sister Charlotte defied convention by insisting on telling the truth about Victorian society as she saw it, even though her stories exceeded the bounds of Victorian approval. In her novel *Jane Eyre,* for example—which she published under the pseudonym Currer Bell—Brontë conveys the frustrations of Victorian women through Jane's outspoken monologue in chapter 12:

Women are supposed to be very calm generally: but women feel just as men feel; they need exercise for their faculties, and a field for their efforts much as their brothers do; they suffer from too rigid a restraint, too absolute a stagnation, precisely as men would suffer; and it is narrow-minded in their more privileged fellow-creatures to say that they ought to confine themselves to making puddings and knitting stockings, or playing on the piano and embroidering bags. It is thoughtless to condemn them, or laugh at them, if they seek to do more

Write Well or Be Silent

❦

In volume 3 of *The Woman Question: Society and Literature in Britain and America, 1837–1883,* Elizabeth K. Helsinger, Robin Lauterbach Sheets, and William Veeder reprint "Silly Novels by Lady Novelists," an essay that George Eliot (Mary Ann Evans) published anonymously in the *Westminister Review* in 1856. In the excerpt, she urges women to achieve high literary standards for their novels or be silent.

"Be not a baker if your head be made of butter," says a homely proverb, which, being interpreted, may mean, let no woman rush into print who is not prepared for the consequences. . . . For it must be plain to every one who looks impartially and extensively into feminine literature, that its greatest deficiencies are due hardly more to the want of intellectual power than to the want of those moral qualities that contribute to literary excellence—patient diligence, a sense of the responsibility involved in publication, and an appreciation of the sacredness of the writer's art. In the majority of women's books you see that kind of facility which springs from the absence of any high standard; that fertility in imbecile combination or feeble imitation which a little self-criticism would check and reduce to barrenness; just as with a total want of musical ear people will sing out of tune, while a degree more melodic sensibility would suffice to render them silent. . . . In novel-writing there are no barriers for incapacity to stumble against, no external criteria to prevent a writer from mistaking foolish facility for mastery. And so we have again and again the old story of La Fontaine's ass, who puts his nose to the flute, and finding that he elicits some sound, exclaims, "Moi, aussi, je joue de la flute" ["I, too, can play the flute"]:—a fable which we commend, at parting, to the consideration of any feminine reader who is in danger of adding to the number of "silly novels by lady novelists."

or learn more than custom has pronounced necessary for their sex. [100]

Brontë was surprised and relieved that the novel gained instant popularity with readers and critics, who praised it for its emotional power and passion, for its outspoken challenges to social convention, and for its attacks on religious hypocrisy. When the critics discovered that "Currer Bell" was actually a woman, their reviews became less favorable.

Like the Brontë sisters, Mary Ann Evans chose to ignore Victorian conventions and the tastes of mass audiences. Between 1858 and 1872, Evans, writing under the pseudonym George Eliot, published four major novels: *Adam Bede, The Mill on the Floss, Silas Marner,* and *Middlemarch.*

Writers for Weeklies and Magazines

Unlike novelists, who worried about their art and their critics, women who wrote short pieces for newspaper weeklies and other periodicals were most concerned with earning a little extra money for their families. These popular periodicals gave women writers new outlets for both fiction and nonfiction. Because much of the material was published anonymously, it is hard to distinguish what was written by women and what by men. Women were most likely the authors of articles whose themes were about morality, romantic love, family, motherhood, and homemaking.

Women, however, wrote sensational stories, either fictional or true, for publication in periodicals. They also wrote full-length novels serialized over three or more weeks in newspapers or magazines. They used titles such as "The Adventures of a Lady's Maid" to get the readers' attention. Gleadle notes that women's

emotions were tapped into by stupendously successful authors of sensationalist fiction such as Mrs. Henry Wood and Mary E. Braddon. Their novels, which told of the dull inanity of middle-class domesticity and the lure of sexual passion, spoke to the emotional needs of women whose expectations of personal fulfillment were growing ever higher. [101]

Popular magazines like this one gave many women writers outlets for both fiction and nonfiction.

There were periodicals whose entire purpose was to provide a forum for religious works. Reformer Mrs. S.C. Hall established a newspaper, as scholar Martha Vicinus says, "in an attempt to fill the demand for cheap reading with something which was scrupulously wholesome and which had a religious, moral, or economic product to sell." [102] In her newspaper, women could publish articles, for example, about the weaknesses of women and how to avoid scandal or unwanted flirtation.

Advice from a Penny Weekly

In *The Ruined Maid: Modes and Manners of Victorian Women,* Geoffrey Eley reprints advice from a penny weekly. This anonymous article advising women not to wear garters was likely written by a woman.

The worst method for supporting stockings that can be adopted, is to place a tight elastic band, or to tie a piece of tape or skein of wool, tightly round the leg just below the knee-joint. This tight band compresses the blood-vessels, and by so doing is productive of much mischief. By checking the flow of blood through the arteries to the lower part of the leg and foot it causes coldness of the feet; by impeding the circulation it produces chilblains [swelling or soreness due to exposure to cold]; and by hampering the return of the blood from the foot and leg through the veins towards the heart, it causes varicose veins—a complaint unfortunately as common as it is painful.

Garters of the ordinary sort should be abolished. If there is a good calf to the leg, and woolen drawers or combinations fitting round the leg are worn, no artificial support is required, as the stockings, presumable also woolen, can be pulled up over the bottoms of the drawers to their full length, and will in that position be supported by friction. This is doubtless the best way of supporting them; but if the leg is thin, or, in the case of children, where it is as yet unformed, suspenders may be worn.

Suspenders are fastened with clips or on to buttons on the outside of the leg, up which they run to the hip-bone, where they are best fastened on to buttons on the bodice used for the support of the other clothing, or on to a broadish band passing round the body, and supported on the hip-bones. A very excellent and still more simple plan however, is to sew two buttons on to the front of the stocking, so as to come one each side just below the bone of the knee cap.

Other women writers used newspapers and magazines to publish advice for other women on topics ranging from relations with husbands to child rearing to cooking to housework. Advice columns were popular with middle-class readers who were urged to seek instruction for their roles as wife, mother, and homemaker. Some advice columns were serious while others adopted a humorous tone. For example, one article advised women to check a man's pockets to see if he was a bachelor or a married man. A bachelor's pocket will contain "a lot of invitations to dances, dinners, and receptions. A tiny glove scented with violet." A married man's pocket will contain "a shopping list ranging from a box of blacking to three yards of lace. Bills. More bills." [103] Women could also publish advice on how to make children sit still in church, their favorite foreign and domestic recipes, and household hints, such as "rats will leave a house in which a guinea-pig is allowed to wander about." [104]

Other women wrote correspondence columns in which readers asked questions about social situations and about romantic concerns. Some newspapers published both the question and the answer; for example, in one column a reader named Pauline asked, how long a daughter should wear mourning for her father. She received a short answer amounting to nine months. Other newspapers published only the answer, but the question was obvious. For example, the servant identified as "Funny Goose" was advised to stop letting her master kiss her when she did something that pleased him. "Misunderstood" was advised to write to the man she loves, admit her mistake, and ask for forgiveness.

Finally, women started their own literary magazines that published serious essays and arguments that concerned the reform movement. There were several, such as the *Englishwomans Review, Victoria Magazine,* and *Women's Suffrage Journal.* Harriet Martineau and Frances Power Cobbe, for example, regularly published essays on economics, religion, political developments, morality, education, and suffrage. These magazines gave women writers a voice and bolstered readers' confidence in reform. George Eliot (Mary Ann Evans) expressed her support when she sent a letter to the editor of the *English Women's Journal:*

> For my own taste, I should say, the more business you can get into the journal—the more statements of philanthropic movements and social facts, and the less *literature,* the better. Not because I like philanthropy and hate literature, but because I want to *know* about philanthropy and don't care for second-rate literature. [105]

It is not clear exactly why Victorian women wrote in such large volumes on such a variety of topics in such a variety of forms. From a modern perspective, it seems understandable, however, that women whose lives were restricted socially and intellectually would find writing a satisfying outlet.

Notes

Introduction: The Strength and Grit of Victorian Women

1. Richard D. Altick, *Victorian People and Ideas.* New York: W. W. Norton, 1973, p. 58.

Chapter 1: The Middle Class Determines Ideal Roles for Women

2. Joan Perkin, *Victorian Women.* New York: New York University Press, 1993, p. 74.
3. Perkin, *Victorian Women,* p. 86.
4. Quoted in Carol Bauer and Lawrence Ritt, eds., *Free and Ennobled: Source Readings in the Development of Victorian Feminism.* Oxford, UK: Pergamon, 1979, p. 13.
5. Quoted in Perkin, *Victorian Women,* p. 1.
6. Quoted in Sally Mitchell, ed., *Victorian Britain: An Encyclopedia.* New York: Garland, 1988, p. 175.
7. Deborah Gorham, *The Victorian Girl and the Feminine Ideal.* Bloomington: Indiana University Press, 1982, p. 65.
8. Quoted in Gorham, *The Victorian Girl and the Feminine Ideal,* p. 70.
9. Quoted in Janet Horowitz Murray, *Strong-Minded Women and Other Lost Voices from Nineteenth-Century England.* New York: Pantheon, 1982, pp. 93–94.
10. Quoted in Murray, *Strong-Minded Women,* p. 147.
11. Quoted in Murray, *Strong-Minded Women,* pp. 24–25.
12. Quoted in Geoffrey Eley, *The Ruined Maid: Modes and Manners of Victorian Women.* Hertfordshire, UK: Priory, 1970, p. 75.
13. Gorham, *The Victorian Girl and the Feminine Ideal,* p. 68.
14. Quoted in Gorham, *The Victorian Girl and the Feminine Ideal,* p. 18.
15. Quoted in Perkin, *Victorian Women,* p. 18.
16. Jane Lewis, *Women in England, 1870–1950: Sexual Divisions and Social Change.* Bloomington: Indiana University Press, 1984, p. 113.
17. Quoted in Murray, *Strong-Minded Women,* pp. 125–26.
18. Quoted in Murray, *Strong-Minded Women,* p. 91.

Chapter 2: Women as Pieceworkers and Shopkeepers

19. Jane Lewis, ed., *Labour and Love: Women's Experience of Home and Family, 1850–1940.* Oxford, UK: Basil Blackwell, 1986, p. 230.

20. Quoted in Perkin, *Victorian Women,* p. 171.
21. Quoted in Murray, *Strong-Minded Women,* p. 355.
22. Quoted in Perkin, *Victorian Women,* p. 189.
23. Quoted in M. Phillips and W.S. Tomkinson, *English Women in Life and Letters.* New York: Benjamin Blom, 1971, p. 392.
24. Quoted in Lewis, *Labour and Love,* p. 203.
25. Quoted in Elizabeth Roberts, *A Woman's Place: An Oral History of Working-Class Women, 1890–1940.* Oxford, UK: Basil Blackwell, 1984, p. 66.
26. Phillips and Tomkinson, *English Women in Life and Letters,* p. 376.
27. Quoted in Phillips and Tomkinson, *English Women in Life and Letters,* p. 381.
28. Eley, *The Ruined Maid,* p. 92.
29. Quoted in Lewis, *Labour and Love,* p. 235.
30. Kathryn Gleadle, *British Women in the Nineteenth Century.* New York: Palgrave, 2001, p. 107.
31. Quoted in Murray, *Strong-Minded Women,* p. 362.
32. Quoted in Mitchell, *Victorian Britain,* p. 763.
33. David Rubinstein, *Before Suffragettes: Women's Emancipation in the 1890s.* New York: St. Martin's, 1986, p. 87.

Chapter 3: Women in a Life of Service

34. Quoted in Pamela Horn, *Victorian Countrywomen.* Oxford, UK: Basil Blackwell, 1991, p. 141.
35. Quoted in Horn, *Victorian Countrywomen,* p. 140.
36. Quoted in Mitchell, *Victorian Britain,* p. 706.
37. Quoted in Mitchell, *Victorian Britain,* p. 378.
38. Perkin, *Victorian Women,* p. 195.
39. Quoted in Horn, *Victorian Countrywomen,* p. 142.
40. Quoted in Roberts, *A Woman's Place,* p. 58.
41. Quoted in Martha Vicinus, ed., *Suffer and Be Still: Women in the Victorian Age.* Bloomington: Indiana University Press, 1972, p. 10.
42. Quoted in Perkin, *Victorian Women,* p. 14.
43. Quoted in Murray, *Strong-Minded Women,* p. 277.
44. Quoted in Horn, *Victorian Countrywomen,* p. 101.
45. Quoted in Perkin, *Victorian Women,* p. 14.
46. Quoted in Perkin, *Victorian Women,* p. 15.
47. Quoted in Horn, *Victorian Countrywomen,* p. 194.
48. Quoted in Mitchell, *Victorian Britain,* p. 552.
49. Quoted in Murray, *Strong-Minded Women,* pp. 305–306.

50. Quoted in Horn, *Victorian Countrywomen,* p. 215.

51. Quoted in Roberts, *A Woman's Place,* p. 107.

52. Quoted in Murray, *Strong-Minded Women,* p. 311.

53. Bauer and Ritt, *Free and Ennobled,* pp. 156–57.

Chapter 4: Woman Employed in Industry

54. Horn, *Victorian Countrywomen,* p. 144.

55. Quoted in Horn, *Victorian Countrywomen,* p. 145.

56. Horn, *Victorian Countrywomen,* pp. 149–50.

57. Quoted in Horn, *Victorian Countrywomen,* p. 153.

58. Horn, *Victorian Countrywomen,* p. 155.

59. Quoted in Horn, *Victorian Countrywomen,* p. 158.

60. Quoted in Horn, *Victorian Countrywomen,* p. 160.

61. Altick, *Victorian People and Ideas,* p. 43.

62. Quoted in Perkin, *Victorian Women,* p. 175.

63. Quoted in Murray, *Strong-Minded Women,* p. 348.

64. Perkin, *Victorian Women,* p. 170.

65. Perkin, *Victorian Women,* p. 193.

66. Quoted in Perkin, *Victorian Women,* p. 192.

67. Quoted in Perkin, *Victorian Women,* p. 198.

68. Perkin, *Victorian Women,* p. 170.

69. Quoted in Katrina Honeyman, *Women, Gender, and Industrialisation in England, 1700–1870.* New York: St. Martin's, 2000, p. 70.

70. Quoted in Murray, *Strong-Minded Women,* p. 373.

Chapter 5: Women Philanthropists and Reformers

71. Quoted in Perkin, *Victorian Women,* p. 166.

72. Perkin, *Victorian Women,* p. 213.

73. Quoted in Bauer and Ritt, *Free and Ennobled,* p. 165.

74. Quoted in Bauer and Ritt, *Free and Ennobled,* pp. 249–50.

75. Quoted in Perkin, *Victorian Women,* p. 44.

76. Quoted in Philippa Levine, *Victorian Feminism, 1850–1900.* Miami: University of Florida Press, 1994, p. 144.

77. Quoted in Levine, *Victorian Feminism,* p. 143.

78. Levine, *Victorian Feminism,* p. 141.

79. Quoted in Perkin, *Victorian Women,* p. 231.

80. Quoted in Bauer and Ritt, *Free and Ennobled,* p. 231.

81. Quoted in Erna Olafson Hellerstein, Leslie Parker Hume, and Karen M. Offen, eds., *Victorian Women: A Documentary Account of Women's Lives in Nineteenth-Century England, France, and the United*

States. Stanford, CA: Stanford University Press, 1981, p. 449.

Chapter 6: Women Entertainers

82. Quoted in Mitchell, *Victorian Britain,* p. 461.
83. Martha Vicinus, ed., *A Widening Sphere: Changing Roles of Victorian Women.* Bloomington: Indiana University Press, 1977, p. 104.
84. Quoted in Kristine Ottesen Garrigan, *Victorian Scandals Representations of Gender and Class.* Athens: Ohio University Press, 1992, pp. 103–104.
85. Quoted in Garrigan, *Victorian Scandals,* p. 106.
86. Quoted in Garrigan, *Victorian Scandals,* p. 101.
87. Quoted in Perkin, *Victorian Women,* p. 221.
88. Perkin, *Victorian Women,* p. 222.
89. Quoted in Perkin, *Victorian Women,* p. 228.

Chapter 7: Women Writers

90. Quoted in Allison Chapman, ed., *Victorian Women Poets.* Rochester, NY: D.S. Brewer, 2003, p. 62.
91. Kathleen Hickok, *Representations of Women: Nineteenth-Century Women's Poetry.* Westport, CT: Greenwood, 1984, p. 182.
92. Elizabeth K. Helsinger, Robin Lauterbach Sheets, and William Veeder, *The Woman Question: Society and Literature in Britain and America,* vol. 3, *Literary Issues, 1837–1883.* New York: Garland, 1983, p. 33.
93. Quoted in Hickok, *Representations of Women,* p. 207.
94. Quoted in Hickok, *Representations of Women,* p. 207.
95. Helsinger, Sheets, and Veeder, *The Woman Question,* p. 51.
96. Quoted in Joanne Shattock, ed., *Women and Literature in Britain, 1800–1900.* Cambridge, UK: Cambridge University Press, 2001, p. 253.
97. Gleadle, *British Women in the Nineteenth Century,* p. 55.
98. Muriel Masefield, *Women Novelists from Fanny Burney to George Eliot.* Freeport, NY: Books for Libraries, 1934, p. 151.
99. Shattock, *Women and Literature in Britain, 1800–1900,* p. 43.
100. Quoted in Shattock, *Women and Literature in Britain, 1800–1900,* pp. 88–89.
101. Gleadle, *British Women in the Nineteenth Century,* p. 176.
102. Vicinus, *A Widening Sphere,* p. 37.
103. Eley, *The Ruined Maid,* p. 26.
104. Eley, *The Ruined Maid,* p. 110.
105. Quoted in Shattock, *Women and Literature in Britain, 1800–1900,* p. 101.

For Further Reading

Books

Ralph A. Bellas, *Christina Rossetti.* Boston: Twayne, 1977. This book includes chapters covering "Goblin Market," the sonnets, religious prose and poetry, and children's poems.

Margaret Howard Blom, *Charlotte Brontë.* Boston: Twayne, 1977. Chapters feature Brontë's life, her unpublished works, and a chapter each on her four major novels are included.

Hector Bolitho, *The Reign of Queen Victoria.* New York: Macmillan, 1948. This biography depicts the queen and her times.

Emily Brontë, *A Peculiar Music: Poems for Young Readers.* Ed. Naomi Lewis, New York: Macmillan, 1971. Besides twenty-nine short poems, the collection has a biographical sketch of Brontë, analysis of her poems, and some of her diary letters.

John W. Deery, *A Short History of Nineteenth-Century England.* London: Blandford, 1963. An account of key social changes and political reforms of the century.

Frank E. Huggett, *A Day in the Life of a Victorian Factory Worker.* London: George Allen & Unwin, 1973. This book portrays the city family in their work, entertainment, school, parental roles, food, pubs, and fairs.

———, *A Day in the Life of a Victorian Farm Worker.* London: George Allen & Unwin, 1975. This work portrays social and family life, work, school, the cottage, food, and entertainment of hired farmworkers.

W.D. Hussey, *British History, 1815–1839.* Cambridge, UK: Cambridge University Press, 1971. A history of developments leading up to Victoria's reign and their effects still felt after her reign.

G.E. Mingay, ed., *The Victorian Countryside.* Vol. 2. New York: Routledge & Kegan Paul, 1981. This collection of short essays covers a variety of rural topics, such as land, country towns, and laboring life, and is accompanied by abundant photographs.

Margorie Quennell and C.H.B. Quennell, *A History of Everyday Things in England: The Rise of Industrialism, 1733–1851.* London: B.T. Batsford, 1934. A history of common items used in Victorian households and illustrated with black-and-white drawings.

———, *A History of Everyday Things in England, 1851–1914.* London: B.T.

Batsford, 1934. A companion volume to the Quennells's other history text, similarly illustrated.

Virginia L. Radley, *Elizabeth Barrett Browning*. New York: Twayne, 1972. Chapters cover Browning's life, early poems, letters, sonnets, politics, and *Aurora Leigh*.

W.J. Reader, *Victorian England*. New York: G.P. Putnam's Sons, 1973. An illustrated history focusing on social classes, especially the working class.

Diane Yancey, *Life in Charles Dickens's England*. San Diego: Lucent, 1999. This book offers a vivid glimpse of life in early Victorian England.

Web Sites

The Victorian Period (www.britain express.com). This site provides information on many aspects of Victorian life, including an overview of Victorian England, Victorian occupations, and Victorian literature.

The Victorian Web (www.victorian web.org). This site provides the article "Christina Rossetti: An Overview," offering information on her life and analysis of her poems, as well as links to sites that cover a host of Victorian social customs.

Works Consulted

Richard D. Altick, *Victorian People and Ideas.* New York: W.W. Norton, 1973. A readable history that provides social and intellectual background on Victorian literature.

Carol Bauer and Lawrence Ritt, eds., *Free and Ennobled: Source Readings in the Development of Victorian Feminism.* Oxford, UK: Pergamon, 1979. A collection of lengthy reprints of documents, reports, and articles about the social and political issues relevant to feminism, covering such topics as work, crime, education, and suffrage.

Alison Chapman, ed., *Victorian Women Poets.* Rochester, NY: D.S. Brewer, 2003. A collection of literary essays written by women, focusing either on a major poet or on themes and forms of women poets.

Geoffrey Eley, *The Ruined Maid: Modes and Manners of Victorian Women.* Hertfordshire, UK: Priory, 1970. A variety of short pieces, advertisements, and illustrations collected from the magazine *Woman's Life,* which was published during the nineteenth century.

Kristine Ottesen Garrigan, *Victorian Scandals: Representations of Gender and Class.* Athens: Ohio University Press, 1992. A collection of essays about Victorian women's issues, such as divorce, discrimination, gambling, and infanticide.

Kathryn Gleadle, *British Women in the Nineteenth Century.* New York: Palgrave, 2001. A discussion of work, politics, and family life of working- and middle-class women, 1800–1860 in the first part, 1860–1890 in the second part.

Deborah Gorham, *The Victorian Girl and Feminine Ideal.* Bloomington: Indiana University Press, 1982. An analysis of the expectation of the middle-class Victorian girl, how she was trained, and what she experienced.

Erna Olafson Hellerstein, Leslie Parker Hume, and Karen M. Offen, eds., *Victorian Women: A Documentary Account of Women's Lives in Nineteenth-Century England, France, and the United States.* Stanford, CA: Stanford University Press, 1981.

Elizabeth K. Helsinger, Robin Lauterbach Sheets, and William Veeder, *The Woman Question: Society and Literature in Britain and America.* Vol. 3. *Literary Issues, 1837–1883.* New York: Garland, 1983. A literary history of Victorian poets, novelists, and essayists, organized around themes.

Kathleen Hickok, *Representations of Women: Nineteenth-Century Women's Poetry.* Westport, CT: Greenwood, 1984. Chapters are organized around women at different stages, such as daughters, spinsters, and New Women, with chapters on Elizabeth Barrett Browning and Christina Rossetti.

Katrina Honeyman, *Women, Gender, and Industrialisation in England, 1700–1870.* New York: St. Martin's, 2000. A history covering the entire period of the Industrial Revolution, explaining how women contributed and how their lives changed economically and socially.

Pamela Horn, *Victorian Countrywomen.* Oxford, UK: Basil Blackwell, 1991. A history of Victorian women from rural areas and villages, addressing social and work issues of women from all classes. An appendix of primary documents shows trends in matters such as birth and death rates and demographics.

Philippa Levine, *Victorian Feminism, 1850–1900.* Miami: University of Florida Press, 1994. A history of feminist issues such as education, politics, and marriage, in relation to Victorian values and practices.

Jane Lewis, *Women in England, 1870–1950: Sexual Divisions and Social Change.* Bloomington: Indiana University Press, 1984. This book begins at the outset of real social changes for women and traces the changes into the next century.

Jane Lewis, ed., *Labour and Love: Women's Experience of Home and Family, 1850–1940.* Oxford, UK: Basil Blackwell, 1986. A collection of essays by various authors that focuses on the personal experiences of women and girls in daily life, work, and marriage.

Muriel Masefield, *Women Novelists from Fanny Burney to George Eliot.* Freeport, NY: Books for Libraries, 1934. An analysis of eleven women novelists that focuses on theme and form and provides a short biographical sketch of each.

Sally Mitchell, ed., *Victorian Britain: An Encyclopedia.* New York: Garland, 1988. This work contains more than eight hundred pages of short essays about important Victorian people, work, social practices, entertainment, and culture. Each essay is written by a scholar in the field.

Janet Horowitz Murray, *Strong-Minded Women and Other Lost Voices from Nineteenth-Century England.* New York: Pantheon, 1982. A collection of Victorian primary documents covering women's personal lives, standards of living, education, work, and prostitution.

Joan Perkin, *Victorian Women.* New York: New York University Press, 1993. An overview of Victorian women, describing their roles, legal rights, work, and political and social activism. It contains many firsthand accounts.

M. Phillips and W.S. Tomkinson, *English Women in Life and Letters.* New York: Benjamin Blom, 1971. A historical account of seventeenth-, eighteenth-, and early-nineteenth-century British women, their fashion, their work, and their daily lives.

K.D. Reynolds, *Aristocratic Women and Political Society in Victorian Britain.* Oxford, UK: Clarendon, 1998. A history focusing entirely on the upper class and the contribution its members made to church, philanthropy, and politics.

Elizabeth Roberts, *A Woman's Place: An Oral History of Working-Class Women, 1890–1940.* Oxford, UK: Basil Blackwell, 1984. Working women's oral accounts of childhood, home-making, and family life.

David Rubinstein, *Before the Suffragettes: Women's Emancipation in the 1890s.* New York: St. Martin's, 1986. After describing the images of women and their work, the book focuses on the women of the 1890s as they fought for freedom and education.

Joanne Shattock, ed., *Women and Literature in Britain, 1800–1900.* Cambridge, UK: Cambridge University Press, 2001. A collection of thirteen essays covering various themes related to literature, such as feminism, domestic writing, poets, theater, and children's literature.

Martha Vicinus, ed., *Suffer and Be Still: Women in the Victorian Age.* Blooming-ton: Indiana University Press, 1972. A collection of essays by woman writers focusing on work, entertainment, and women's personal and sexual issues.

———, *A Widening Sphere: Changing Roles of Victorian Women.* Blooming-ton: Indiana University Press, 1977. A collection of essays by women writers covering social issues such as woman's rights, prostitution, education, theater, and publishing.

Index

Achurch, Janet, 77

Acton, William, 81–82

actresses, 76–80

Adam Bede (Evans), 93

agriculture gangs, 50–53

Alexandra Magazine, 66

Altick, Richard D., 9, 54

Anderson, Elizabeth Garrett, 46

Argyll Room, 83

Ashton, Rose, 38

Ashwell, Lena, 77

Aurora Leigh (Browning), 87–88

Bancroft, Squire, 76

Bartolozzi, Lucy Elizabeth. *See* Vestris, Madame

Bauer, Carol, 14, 46

Bedford College, 68

Beethoven, Ludwig van, 74

Beeton, Isabella, 16, 19

Benson, John, 30

Bentley, Elizabeth, 55

Besant, Annie Wood, 16, 54, 65–66, 83

Blackwood's Edinburgh Magazine, 84

Board of Poor Law Guardians, 71

Bodichon, Barbara Leigh Smith, 63, 69

Boucherett, Jessie, 63

"Boy in the Gallery, The" (song), 75

Braddon, Mary E., 93

Bright, Ursula, 70

British Ladies Lying in Institution, 45

British Women in the Nineteenth Century (Gleadle), 27

Brontë, Charlotte, 40, 42, 90–92

Brontë, Emily, 90–91

Browning, Elizabeth Barrett, 85–88

Bryant and May (company), 65

Burrows, Mrs., 50

Butler, Josephine, 71

Carpenter, Mary, 62

Chamberlain, Mary, 44

Chamber's Journal (periodical), 66–67

"Characteristics of Husbands" (Ellis), 22

charwomen, 36

children

    agriculture gangs and, 53

    as factory workers, 54–57

    gender teaching of, 18–19

    health concerns and, 15–16

    mining and, 58–59

    morality teachings of, 17–18

    Newgate Prison and, 62

    religious teachings of, 16–17

    as textile workers, 54

clothing, 13–14

Cobbe, Frances Power, 69–70, 95

Cobbett, William, 25–26

Contagious Diseases Acts, 70–71

Cooper, Anthony Ashley, 57

Corbett, Joseph, 56

courtesans, 81–82

Covent Garden, 33, 73, 82

Cranfield (Gaskell), 89

Cuffe, Sybil, 41

Currer Bell. *See* Brontë, Charlotte

Dalrymple, John, 28

Davies, Margaret Llewelyn, 64

Davies, Stella, 19

Davis, Emily, 68

Davis, Tracy C., 78–79

Days' Doings (newspaper), 80

department store, 31

Diary of an Ennuyee, The (Anna Jameson), 22

Dilke, Emilia F.S., 66

Dippenhall (farm), 50–51

doctors, 45–46

domestic service, 6–7

    compensation for, 37–38

    duties/hardships of, 35–37

    governesses and, 38, 40–43

    servants and, 19–20

middle-class and, 34, 38
  upper-class and, 35–36
  working-class and, 34–35, 39
"Domestic Service and Democracy" (Salmon), 37
"Dramatic Doings" (column), 80
Duke of Clarence. *See* William IV

Eastlake, Elizabeth, 38, 40
education
  agriculture gangs and, 53
  argument for, 14
  cottage schools and, 24
  governesses and, 40
  medical students and, 68
  middle-class and, 16–18
  opera/oratorio soloists and, 74
  reformers and, 60, 62, 66–68
  schools for girls and, 42–43
  training loans and, 63
Education Act of 1876, 53
Eley, Geoffrey, 17, 30, 94
Eliot, George, 90, 92–93, 95
Ellis, Sarah Stickney, 11, 19, 22
employment, 63–66
England
  industrialized, map of, 12
  Victorian, map of, 8
English Woman's Journal (periodical), 64, 95
Englishwoman's Review (periodical), 31, 63, 95
English Women in Life & Letters (Phillips, Tomkinson), 25, 42, 56
entertainment
  actresses and, 76–80
  comedy theaters and, 78
  music halls and, 75
  New Women and, 77
  opera and, 73–74
  operettas/oratorios and, 74
  sexual content and, 75, 79
  theater managers, women and, 75–76
Evans, Mary Ann. *See* Eliot, George

factories
  children and, 54–57
  match workers and, 54–55
  pregnancy and, 57
  textile workers and, 54
"Factory Girl, The." *See* Johnston, Ellen
Faggetter, Kate, 34

Faithful, Emily, 63–64
Faithful, Lilian, 68
farms
  agriculture gangs and, 50–53
  employment of wives on, 47–49
  hiring fairs and, 53
  migrant workers and, 49–51, 53
Farr, Florence, 77
Faucit, Helena, 80
Fawcett, Millicent Garrett, 72
Foley, Alice, 54
Fortnightly Review (periodical), 66
Free and Ennobled (Bauer and Ritt), 14
Fry, Elizabeth, 61–62

Gaiety Girls, 79
Gallay, Mary Ann, 52
Gang Act of 1867, 53
Garrigan, Kristine Ottesen, 80
Gaskell, Elizabeth, 89
Gergits, Julia M., 37
Gilbert, William, 74
Gladstone, Mary, 41
Gleadle, Kathryn, 27, 31, 90, 93
"Goblin Market" (Rossetti), 88
Gorham, 19
governesses, 38, 40–43
Governesses' Benevolent Institution, 67
Government Employment Commission, 52
Grey, William, 14

Hall, S.C. (Mrs.), 94
Hamilton, Cicely, 77
Hamilton, Janet, 85
Handel, George, 74
Harrison, Jane Ellen, 40
Heir of Redclyffe, The (Yonge), 89
Helsinger, Elizabeth K., 88–89, 92
Hemans, Felicia, 84
Hickok, Kathleen, 87
H.M.S. Pinafore (Gilbert and Sullivan), 74
Hoffman, Wilson J., 75
Holborn, 83
Horn, Pamela, 47
House of Lords, 70, 78
"Housework and Domestic Technology," (Gergits), 37
"Household Prisoner, The" (Nightingale), 22
"How Women Earn a Living" (article), 30

Ibsen, Henrik, 77
"Image and Reality; The Actress and Society" (Kent), 77
Industrial Revolution, 6
Industrial Schools Acts, 62
Ireley (farm), 48

Jameson, Anna Brownell Murphy, 22
Jameson, Robert, 22
Jane Eyre (Charlotte Brontë), 91
Jefferies, Richard, 48
Jex-Blake, Sophia, 46
Johnston, Ellen, 85
Jordan, Dorothy, 82

Kelly, Fanny, 80
Kendal, Madge Robertson, 80
Kent, Christopher, 77
Kershaw, Patience, 59
Kingston, Gertrude, 77

Ladies' Association for the Improvement of Female Prisoners, 62
Langham Place Circle, 63
Lantry, Lily, 78
La Scala, 73
"Letters to Women on Money Earning" (Parkes), 66
Levine, Phillipa, 45, 66, 68, 70
Lewis, Jane, 20, 23, 26
Lewis, Sarah, 16
Life as We Have Known It (Burrows), 50
Lloyd, Marie, 75
London Medical College for Women, 46
London's New Hospital for Women and Children, 46

Married Women's Property Act, 70
Martineau, Harriet, 70, 95
Mary Barton; A Tale of a Manchester Life (Gaskell), 89
Masefield, Muriel, 90
Matrimonial Causes Act, 70
Mayhew, Henry, 83
McCarthy, Lillah, 77
Melba, Nellie, 73–74
Mendelssohn, Felix, 74
Metropolitan Opera, 73
middle-class
    clothing and, 13–14
    entertainment and, 73–74, 76, 78

philanthropy and, 60–62
poetry and, 85
prostitution and, 83
religion and, 16–17
writing and, 84, 89–90
    see also middle-class wives
middle-class wives
    health care for children and, 15–16
    homemaker role of, 19–22
    sexual ignorance of, 11
    submissiveness of, 10–11
    teaching roles of, 16–18
    upholding wealthy image and, 11, 13–15
Middlemarch (Eliot), 93
midwives, 45–46
migrant workers, 49–51, 53
Mill on the Floss, The (Eliot), 93
mining, 6–7, 58–59
Mitchell, Sally, 35
More, Hannah, 60
More, Martha, 60
Munby, Arthur, 52
Murray, Janet Horowitz, 50, 61, 82
music halls, 75

National Association for the Promotion of Social Science, 80
Newgate Prison, 61–62
New Women, 77
Nightingale, Florence, 22, 43–45
Norton, Caroline, 69–70
Norton, George, 69–70
Novello, Clara, 74
novels. See writing
nursing, 43–44

Obstetrical Society, 45
Olympic Theater, 75–76
"On Governesses" (Eastlake), 40
opera, 73–74
operettas, 74
oratorios, 74

Paine, Eva, 23–24
Pankhurst, Emmeline, 71–72
Parkes, Bessie Rayner, 63, 66, 69
Parliament
    child custody and, 70
    factory work and, 54–56

mining and, 59
poor mothers and, 64
protection laws and, 7, 9
suffrage and, 71
women's rights and, 69–70
Patterson, Emma, 64–66
Pembrokeshire, 58
penny capitalists, 24–25
Penny Capitalists (Benson), 30
Perkin, Joan, 10, 19, 37, 58, 81
philanthropy, 60, 62–63, 66–68
Phillips, M., 25, 27, 42, 56
"Piccadilly Trot, The" (song), 75
piecework
    dressmaking, 26–29
        apprentices in, 27–29
        sweatshops and, 28
    fly tying, 29–30
    miscellaneous forms of, 27, 29
    needlework, 23–26
    penny capitalists and, 24–25
Place, Frances, 25
*Plain Letter to the Lord Chancellor on the Infant Custody Bill,
    A* (Caroline Norton), 70
poets, 84–88
Potter, Cora Brown, 78
prima donnas, 83
Prince of Wales, 78
Princess Ida (Gilbert and Sullivan), 74
Prostitutes (Acton), 82
prostitution
    courtesans and, 81–82
    mistresses and, 82
    prima donnas and, 82–83
    sexually transmitted diseases and, 70–71
    thieves' women and, 83
    West End and, 81

Quarterly Review (periodical), 38
"Queen of the Tarts." *See* Wilson, Harriette
Queen's College, 67–68
Queen Victoria, 6–7, 9, 44, 78

Raid, Elizabeth, 68
reformers
    Contagious Diseases Act and, 70–71
    education and, 66–68
    employment and, 63–64
    periodicals and, 95

prostitution and, 80, 83
religion and, 83
social issues and, 61–62, 83, 89
suffrage and, 71–72
trade unions and, 64–66
women's rights and, 68–70
religion
    middle-class and, 16–17
    periodicals and, 94
    reformers and, 83
    writing and, 89
Reynolds, John, 33
Richelieu, Ann, 10
Ritt, Lawrence, 14, 46
Roberts, Elizabeth, 20, 36, 39, 53
Roberts, Sarah Ann, 52
Robins, Elizabeth, 77
Rossetti, Christina, 85–86, 88
Royal London Ophthalmic Hospital, 28
Royal Opera House, 73
"Royal Princess, A" (Rossetti), 88
Rubinstein, David, 33
Ruined Maid: Modes and Manners of Victorian Women, The
    (Eley), 30, 94
Runaway Girl, The (play), 78
Rural Rides (Cobbett), 25
Ruth (Gaskell), 25, 89
Ryan, Michael, 79

Salmon, Edward, 37
Savoy Theater, 74
Seabright, Emma, 48
servants. *See* domestic service
"Servants" (Mitchell), 35
sexually transmitted diseases, 70–71
Shattock, Joanne, 90
Shaw, George Bernard, 77
Sheets, Robin Lauterbach, 89, 92
Shop Girl, The (play), 78
Silas Marner (Eliot), 93
"Silly Novels by Lady Novelists" (essay), 92
Social Science Association, 14
Society for Promoting the Employment of Women,
    63
Sonnets from the Portuguese (Browning), 86
"Street Traders" (Reynolds), 33
*Strong-Minded Women and Other Lost Voices from the Nine-
    teenth Century* (Murray), 50, 61, 82
St. Thomas Hospital, 43

suffrage, 71
suffragettes, 71
Sullivan, Arthur, 74
sweatshops, 28

Thackeray, William, 40
Theatrical Ladies Guild, 77
thieves' women, 83
Toilers of the Field (Jefferies), 48
Tomkinson, W.S., 25, 27, 42, 56
Trade Union Conference (1875), 65
trade unions, 64–66
Trial by Jury (Gilbert and Sullivan), 74

University of Edinburgh (Scotland), 46
University of London, 68
University of the Sorbonne (Paris), 46
upper-class
    domestic service and, 34–35
    entertainment and, 73, 78
    philanthropy and, 62–63

Veeder, William, 89, 92
Vestris, Madame, 75–76
Vicinus, Martha, 77, 94
Victoria Magazine, 32, 44, 64, 95
Victorian era
    beginning/end of, 6
    domestic abuse during, 7, 69–70
    entertainment and, 73
    hardships of, 6
    marriage and, 10
    rights of women during, 7, 9, 68–71, 77
Victorian Feminism (periodical), 45, 66, 68
Victorian People and Ideas (Altick), 54
Victorian Scandals (Garrigan), 80
Victorian Women (Perkin), 10
Victoria Press, 63–64

Walker, Alexander, 11
Ward and Lock's Home Book, 15
West End, 75, 81
West London Express (periodical), 64
Westminster Review (periodical), 92
"White Slavery of London Match Workers, The"
    (Besant), 54, 65
Widening Sphere: Changing Roles of Victorian Women, A
    (Vicinus), 77

"Wife Torture in England" (Cobbe), 70
William IV, (king of Great Britain and Ireland), 82
Wilson, Harriette, 81
Wilson, Marie, 80
Winter Studies and Summer Rambles in Canada (Anna
    Jameson), 22
Wives of England (Ellis), 19
*Woman Questioned: Society and Literature in Britain and
    America, 1837–1883, The* (Helsinger, Sheets, and
    Veeder), 92
Woman's Life (periodical), 30
Woman's Mission (Sarah Lewis), 16
Woman's Place, A (Roberts), 36, 39, 53
Woman's Place: An Oral History of Working-Class Women, A
    (Elizabeth Roberts), 20
Women Guardians' Society, 61
Women Physiologically Considered (Walker), 11
Women's Co-operative Guild, 64
Women's Printing Society, 65
Women's Protective and Provident League, 61, 64
women's rights, 7, 9, 68–71, 77
Women's Social and Political Union, 71
Women's Suffrage Journal (periodical), 95
Women's Union Journal (periodical), 65
Wood, Henry (Mrs.), 93
working-class
    doctors and, 45–46
    domestic service and, 34–35
    entertainment and, 73, 75
    midwives and, 44–45
    nursing and, 43–44
    poets and, 85
    shopkeepers and, 29–32
    Society for Promoting the Employment of Women
        and, 63
    street vendors and, 32–33
World War I, 6, 77
writing
    artistic novels and, 90–93
    domestic novels and, 89–90
    periodicals and, 93–95
    poetry and, 84–88
Wuthering Heights (Emily Brontë), 90

Yewsdale, Betty, 24
Yonge, Charlotte, 89
Youthful Offenders Act of 1854, 62

Picture Credits

Cover Image: © Tate Gallery, London/
   Art Resource, NY
© Archivo Iconografico, S.A./CORBIS,
   35
© Bettmann/CORBIS, 26, 29, 91 (left)
© Christie's Images/CORBIS, 38
© CORBIS, 55, 58
© Fine Art Photographic Library/Art
   Resource, NY, 18, 21, 32, 67, 85
© Fine Art Photographic
   Library/CORBIS, 17
© Giraudon/Art Resource, NY, 48
© Historical Picture Archive/CORBIS,
   76
Hulton/Archive by Getty Images, 86
   (left), 89, 91 (right)

© Hulton–Deutsch Collection/CORBIS,
   69, 86 (right)
© Image Select/Art Resource, NY, 43
© Erich Lessing/Art Resource, NY,
   39
© Mary Evans Picture Library, 60, 62,
   65, 72, 74, 78, 79, 81, 93
© Reunion des Musees Nationaux/Art
   Resource, NY, 24, 51
© Scala/Art Resource, NY, 49
© Smithsonian American Art Museum,
   Washington, DC/Art Resource, NY,
   13
© Victoria & Albert Museum, London/
   Art Resource, NY, 7, 41
Steve Zmina, 8, 12

About the Author

Clarice Swisher is a freelance writer and a former English teacher. She taught English in Minnesota for several years before devoting herself full time to writing. She is the author or editor of more than twenty books, including *The Glorious Revolution, Victorian England,* and *Understanding the Scarlet Letter,* published by Lucent Books, and *The History of Nations: England* and *Galileo,* published by Greenhaven Press. She lives in Saint Paul, Minnesota.